FOUR CORNERS

Second Edition

Student's Book
with Online Self-Study

JACK C. RICHARDS & DAVID BOHLKE

CAMBRIDGE
UNIVERSITY PRESS

CAMBRIDGE
UNIVERSITY PRESS

University Printing House, Cambridge CB2 8BS, United Kingdom

One Liberty Plaza, 20th Floor, New York, NY 10006, USA

477 Williamstown Road, Port Melbourne, VIC 3207, Australia

314–321, 3rd Floor, Plot 3, Splendor Forum, Jasola District Centre, New Delhi – 110025, India

103 Penang Road, #05-06/07, Visioncrest Commercial, Singapore 238467

Cambridge University Press is part of the University of Cambridge.

It furthers the University's mission by disseminating knowledge in the pursuit of education, learning and research at the highest international levels of excellence.

www.cambridge.org
Information on this title: www.cambridge.org/fourcorners

© Cambridge University Press 2012, 2019

First published 2012
Second edition 2019

20 19 18 17 16 15 14 13 12 11 10 9 8 7 6 5

Printed in Great Britain by CPI Group (UK) Ltd, Croydon CR0 4YY

A catalogue record for this publication is available from the British Library

ISBN 978-1-108-55989-8   Student's Book with Online Self-Study 4
ISBN 978-1-108-55990-4   Student's Book with Online Self-Study 4A
ISBN 978-1-108-63118-1   Student's Book with Online Self-Study 4B
ISBN 978-1-108-56025-2   Student's Book with Online Self-Study and Online Workbook 4
ISBN 978-1-108-56029-0   Student's Book with Online Self-Study and Online Workbook 4A
ISBN 978-1-108-56032-0   Student's Book with Online Self-Study and Online Workbook 4B
ISBN 978-1-108-45942-6   Workbook 4
ISBN 978-1-108-45945-7   Workbook 4A
ISBN 978-1-108-45946-4   Workbook 4B
ISBN 978-1-108-64434-1   Teacher's Edition with Complete Assessment Program 4
ISBN 978-1-108-56022-1   Full Contact with Online Self-Study 4
ISBN 978-1-108-56023-8   Full Contact with Online Self-Study 4A
ISBN 978-1-108-56024-5   Full Contact with Online Self-Study 4B
ISBN 978-1-108-45952-5   Presentation Plus Level 4

Additional resources for this publication at www.cambridge.org/fourcorners

Authors' acknowledgments

Many people contributed to the development of *Four Corners*. The authors and publisher would like to particularly thank the following **reviewers**:

Nele Noe, **Academy for Educational Development, Qatar Independent Secondary School for Girls**, Doha, Qatar; Pablo Stucchi, **Antonio Raimondi School** and **Instituto San Ignacio de Loyola**, Lima, Peru; Nadeen Katz, **Asia University**, Tokyo, Japan; Tim Vandenhoek, **Asia University**, Tokyo, Japan; Celso Frade and Sonia Maria Baccari de Godoy, **Associação Alumni**, São Paulo, Brazil; Rosane Bandeira, **Atlanta Idiomas**, Manaus, Brazil; Cacilda Reis da Silva, **Atlanta Idiomas**, Manaus, Brazil; Gretta Sicsu, **Atlanta Idiomas**, Manaus, Brazil; Naila Maria Cañiso Ferreira, **Atlanta Idiomas**, Manaus, Brazil; Hothnã Moraes de Souza Neto, **Atlanta Idiomas**, Manaus, Brazil; Jacqueline Kurtzious, **Atlanta Idiomas**, Manaus, Brazil; José Menezes Ribeiro Neto, **Atlanta Idiomas**, Manaus, Brazil; Sheila Ribeiro Cordeiro, **Atlanta Idiomas**, Manaus, Brazil; Juliana Fernandes, **Atlanta Idiomas**, Manaus, Brazil; Aline Alexandrina da Silva, **Atlanta Idiomas**, Manaus, Brazil; Kari Miller, **Binational Center**, Quito, Ecuador; Alex K. Oliveira, **Boston University**, Boston, MA, USA; Noriko Furuya, **Bunka Gakuen University**, Tokyo, Japan; Robert Hickling, **Bunka Gakuen University**, Tokyo, Japan; John D. Owen, **Bunka Gakuen University**, Tokyo, Japan; Elisabeth Blom, **Casa Thomas Jefferson**, Brasília, Brazil; Lucilena Oliveira Andrade, **Centro Cultural Brasil Estados Unidos (CCBEU Belém)**, Belém, Brazil; Marcelo Franco Borges, **Centro Cultural Brasil Estados Unidos (CCBEU Belém)**, Belém, Brazil; Geysa de Azevedo Moreira, **Centro Cultural Brasil Estados Unidos (CCBEU Belém)**, Belém, Brazil; Anderson Felipe Barbosa Negrão, **Centro Cultural Brasil Estados Unidos (CCBEU Belém)**, Belém, Brazil; Henry Grant, **CCBEU – Campinas**, Campinas, Brazil; Maria do Rosário, **CCBEU – Franca**, Franca, Brazil; Ane Cibele Palma, **CCBEU Inter Americano**, Curitiba, Brazil; Elen Flavia Penques da Costa, **Centro de Cultura Idiomas – Taubaté**, Taubaté, Brazil; Inara Lúcia Castillo Couto, **CEL LEP – São Paulo**, São Paulo, Brazil; Sonia Patricia Cardoso, **Centro de Idiomas Universidad Manuela Beltrán**, Barrio Cedritos, Colombia; Geraldine Itiago Losada, **Centro Universitario Grupo Sol (Musali)**, Mexico City, Mexico; Nick Hilmers, **DePaul University**, Chicago, IL, USA; Monica L. Montemayor Menchaca, **EDIMSA**, Metepec, Mexico; Angela Whitby, **Edu-Idiomas Language School**, Cholula, Puebla, Mexico; Mary Segovia, **El Monte Rosemead Adult School**, Rosemead, CA, USA; Dr. Deborah Aldred, **ELS Language Centers, Middle East Region**, Abu Dhabi, United Arab Emirates; Leslie Lott, **Embassy CES**, Ft. Lauderdale, FL, USA; M. Martha Lengeling, **Escuela de Idiomas**, Guanajuato, Mexico; Pablo Frias, **Escuela de Idiomas UNAPEC**, Santo Domingo, Dominican Republic; Tracy Vanderhoek, **ESL Language Center**, Toronto, Canada; Kris Vicca and Michael McCollister, **Feng Chia University**, Taichung, Taiwan; Flávia Patricia do Nascimento Martins, **First Idiomas**, Sorocaba, Brazil; Andrea Taylor, **Florida State University in Panama**, Panamá, Panama; Carlos Lizárraga González, **Groupo Educativo Angloamericano**, Mexico City, Mexico; Bo-Kyung Lee, **Hankuk University of Foreign Studies**, Seoul, South Korea; Dr. Martin Endley, **Hanyang University**, Seoul, South Korea; Mauro Luiz Pinheiro, **IBEU Ceará**, Ceará, Brazil; Ana Lúcia da Costa Maia de Almeida, **IBEU Copacabana**, Copacabana, Brazil; Maristela Silva, **ICBEU Manaus**, Manaus, Brazil; Magaly Mendes Lemos, **ICBEU São José dos Campos**, São José dos Campos, Brazil; Augusto Pelligrini Filho, **ICBEU São Luis**, São Luis, Brazil; Leonardo Mercado, **ICPNA**, Lima, Peru; Lucia Rangel Lugo, **Instituto Tecnológico de San Luis Potosí**, San Luis Potosí, Mexico; Maria Guadalupe Hernández Lozada, **Instituto Tecnológico de Tlalnepantla**, Tlalnepantla de Baz, Mexico; Karen Stewart, **International House Veracruz**, Veracruz, Mexico; Tom David, **Japan College of Foreign Languages**, Tokyo, Japan;

Andy Burki, **Korea University, International Foreign Language School**, Seoul, South Korea; Jinseo Noh, **Kwangwoon University**, Seoul, South Korea; Neil Donachey, **La Salle Junior and Senior High School**, Kagoshima, Japan; Rich Hollingworth, **La Salle Junior and Senior High School**, Kagoshima, Japan; Quentin Kum, **La Salle Junior and Senior High School**, Kagoshima, Japan; Geoff Oliver, **La Salle Junior and Senior High School**, Kagoshima, Japan; Martin Williams, **La Salle Junior and Senior High School**, Kagoshima, Japan; Nadezhda Nazarenko, **Lone Star College**, Houston, TX, USA; Carolyn Ho, **Lone Star College-Cy-Fair**, Cypress, TX, USA; Kaoru Kuwajima, **Meijo University**, Nogoya, Japan; Alice Ya-fen Chou, **National Taiwan University of Science and Technology**, Taipei, Taiwan; Raymond Dreyer, **Northern Essex Community College**, Lawrence, MA, USA; Mary Keter Terzian Megale, **One Way Línguas-Suzano**, São Paulo, Brazil; B. Greg Dunne, **Osaka Shoin Women's University**, Higashi-Osaka, Japan; Robert Maran, **Osaka Shoin Women's University**, Higashi-Osaka, Japan; Bonnie Cheeseman, **Pasadena Community College** and **UCLA American Language Center**, Los Angeles, CA, USA; Simon Banha, **Phil Young's English School**, Curitiba, Brazil; Oh Jun Il, **Pukyong National University**, Busan, South Korea; Carmen Gehrke, **Quatrum English Schools**, Porto Alegre, Brazil; John Duplice, **Rikkyo University**, Tokyo, Japan; Wilzania da Silva Nascimento, **Senac**, Manaus, Brazil; Miva Silva Kingston, **Senac**, Manaus, Brazil; Lais Lima, **Senac**, Manaus, Brazil; Yuan-hsun Chuang, **Soo Chow University**, Taipei, Taiwan; Mengjiao Wu, **Shanghai Maritime University**, Shanghai, China; Wen hsiang Su, **Shih Chien University Kaohsiung Campus**, Kaohsiung, Taiwan; Lynne Kim, **Sun Moon University (Institute for Language Education)**, Cheon An City, Chung Nam, South Korea; Regina Ramalho, **Talken English School**, Curitiba, Brazil; Tatiana Mendonça, **Talken English School**, Curitiba, Brazil; Ricardo Todeschini, **Talken English School**, Curitiba, Brazil; Monica Carvalho da Rocha, **Talken English School**, Joinville, Brazil; Karina Schoene, **Talken English School**, Joinville, Brazil; Diaña Peña Munoz and Zira Kuri, **The Anglo**, Mexico City, Mexico; Christopher Modell, **Tokai University**, Tokyo, Japan; Song-won Kim, **TTI (Teacher's Training Institute)**, Seoul, South Korea; Nancy Alarcón, **UNAM FES Zaragoza Language Center**, Mexico City, Mexico; Laura Emilia Fierro López, **Universidad Autónoma de Baja California**, Mexicali, Mexico; María del Rocío Domínguez Gaona, **Universidad Autónoma de Baja California**, Tijuana, Mexico; Saul Santos Garcia, **Universidad Autónoma de Nayarit**, Nayarit, Mexico; Christian Meléndez, **Universidad Católica de El Salvador**, San Salvador, El Salvador; Irasema Mora Pablo, **Universidad de Guanajuato**, Guanajuato, Mexico; Alberto Peto, **Universidad de Oaxaca**, Tehuantepec, Mexico; Carolina Rodriguez Beltan, **Universidad Manuela Beltrán, Centro Colombo Americano**, and **Universidad Jorge Tadeo Lozano**, Bogotá, Colombia; Nidia Milena Molina Rodriguez, **Universidad Manuela Beltrán** and **Universidad Militar Nueva Granada**, Bogotá, Colombia; Yolima Perez Arias, **Universidad Nacional de Colombia**, Bogotá, Colombia; Héctor Vázquez García, **Universidad Nacional Autónoma de Mexico**, Mexico City, Mexico; Pilar Barrera, **Universidad Técnica de Ambato**, Ambato, Ecuador; Doborah Hulston, **University of Regina**, Regina, Canada; Rebecca J. Shelton, **Valparaiso University, Interlink Language Center**, Valparaiso, IN, USA; Tae Lee, **Yonsei University**, Seodaemun-gu, Seoul, South Korea; Claudia Thereza Nascimento Mendes, **York Language Institute**, Rio de Janeiro, Brazil; Jamila Jenny Hakam, **ELT Consultant**, Muscat, Oman; Stephanie Smith, **ELT Consultant**, Austin, TX, USA.

Scope and sequence

LEVEL 4B	Learning outcomes	Grammar	Vocabulary
Unit 7 Pages 63–72			

New ways of thinking
A *Inventions*
B *Got any suggestions?*
 	
C *Accidental inventions*
D *Making life easier*
	Students can . . .
	☑ describe important inventions
	☑ elicit ideas
	☑ suggesting solutions
	☑ discuss how things have been improved
	☑ describe something they invented
		So and *such*
		The passive
			Positive and negative
			  descriptions
			Verb and noun
			  formation

Unit 8 Pages 73–82			

Lessons in life
A *Why did I do that?*
B *I'm sure you'll do fine.*
 	
C *What if . . . ?*
D *A day to remember*
	Students can . . .
	☑ describe events in the past
	☑ express worry
	☑ reassure someone
	☑ talk about how things might have been
	☑ describe a memorable day
		Past perfect
		Third conditional
			Prefixes: *mis-*, *dis-*,
			  and *re-*
			Expression with
			  make and *get*

Unit 9 Pages 83–92			
Can you believe it? A *Everyday explanations* B *I'm pretty sure that . . .* C *History's mysteries* D *Unexplained abilities*	Students can . . . ☑ speculate about everyday situations ☑ express probability and improbability ☑ ask and speculate about historical events ☑ discuss the power of memory	Past modals for speculating Embedded questions	Suffixes *-ful* and *-less* Mysterious events
Unit 10 Pages 93–102			

Perspectives
A *A traffic accident*
B *As I was saying . . .*
C *There's always an explanation*
D *Seeing things differently*
	Students can . . .
	☑ report what people say
	☑ change and return to the topic
	☑ report what people ask
	☑ discuss different perspectives
		Reported statements
		Reported *yes* / *no*
		  questions
			Three-word phrasal
			  verbs
			Verbs + prepositions

Unit 11 Pages 103–112			
The real world A *Getting it done* B *Let me see . . .* C *Future goals* D *My career*	Students can . . . ☑ talk about getting things done ☑ take time to think in an interview ☑ close an interview ☑ ask and talk about future goals ☑ discuss future careers	Causative *get* and *have* Future continuous vs. future with *will*	Word partners Setting goals
Unit 12 Pages 113–122			

Finding solutions
A *Environmental concerns*
B *That's a good point.*
C *My community*
D *Getting involved*
	Students can . . .
	☑ discuss environmental trends
	☑ support and not support an opinion
	☑ discuss ways to improve their community
	☑ discuss ways to raise awareness
		Present continuous
		  passive
		Infinitive passive
		Linking words
			Preventing pollution
			Community
			  improvement

Functional language	Listening and Pronunciation	Reading and Writing	Speaking
Interactions: Eliciting an idea Suggesting a solution	**Listening:** Unusual solutions to unusual problems i-Cybie, a robot dog **Pronunciation:** Emphatic stress	**Reading:** "Technology Helps Japan's Elderly" An article **Writing:** An Invention	• Discussion of inventions • *Keep talking:* Promoting creative products • Vote on inventive solutions • Discussion of improvements to early innovations • *Keep talking:* Discussion of product improvements • Description of an original invention
Interactions: Expressing worry Reassuring someone	**Listening:** Worrisome situations Memorable days **Pronunciation:** Reduction of had	**Reading:** "Tuesday, January 9, 2007" A magazine article **Writing:** About a memorable day	• Information exchange about past experiences • *Keep talking:* Picture story • Role play about difficult situations • Description of personal experiences that might have been different • *Keep talking:* Discussion of possible outcomes in different situations • Description of a memorable day
Interactions: Expressing probability Expressing improbability	**Listening:** Mind-reading "The Magpies and the Bell," a South Korean folktale **Pronunciation:** Intonation in embedded questions	**Reading:** "The Woman Who Can't forget" A magazine article **Writing:** An origin myth	• Discussion of possible explanations for unusual everyday events • *Keep talking:* Speculations about pictured events • Information exchange about probability • Discussion of possible explanations for historical mysteries • *Keep talking:* Descriptions and speculations about unsolved mysteries • Story-telling from different cultures
Interactions: Changing the topic Returning to a topic	**Listening:** Three conversations about sports Interview for the Proust Questionnaire **Pronunciation:** Linked vowel sounds with / w / and / y /	**Reading:** "The Dress" A lecture **Writing:** Questionnaire results	• "Whisper the sentence" game to report what people say • *Keep talking:* "Find the differences" activity about eyewitness reports • Discussion about sports • "Find someone who" activity about famous people • *Keep talking:* Survey about general topics • Questionnaire about thoughts and values
Interactions: Taking time to think Closing an interview	**Listening:** Plans to get things done A job interview **Pronunciation:** Reduction of will	**Reading:** "Jobs of the future" An article **Writing:** A letter of interest	• Discussion about ways to prepare for an interview • *Keep talking:* Match the places and the activities • Role play about a job interview • Discussion of future goals • *Keep talking:* Survey about life in the future
Interactions: Supporting an opinion Not supporting an opinion	**Listening:** Bottled water and the environment How people help solve community issues **Pronunciation:** Rise-falling and low falling tones	**Reading:** "El Sistema: Social Change Through Music" A magazine article **Writing:** A letter to a community leader	• Discussion of environmental trends • *Keep talking:* Board game about the environment • Comparison of opinions about issues • Discussion about ways to improve the quality of life of people in the community • *Keep talking:* A plan for a community improvement project • Information exchange about raising awareness

Classroom Language

A 🎧 **Complete the conversations with the correct sentences. Then listen and check your answers.**

> Do you think this is correct?
> ✓ Do you want to join our group?
> I'm sorry for being late.
>
> Is it all right if I . . .
> Which number are we on?
> Would you mind explaining that to me?

1
A <u>Do you want to join our group?</u>

B That'd be great. Thanks.

2
A _____

B Sure. I think I understand it.

3
A _____
_____
leave five minutes early tomorrow?
I have a doctor's appointment.

B Of course.

4
A _____
My last class ended late.

B That's OK. Take your seat.

5
A _____

B We just finished question two, so we're on number three now.

6
A _____

B I don't think so. I think you need to use the past tense here.

B `PAIR WORK` **Practice the conversations.**

7 New ways of thinking

Warm Up

A Look at the pictures. What do you see?

B What problem did each of these creations try to solve? Do you think they were successful?

A Inventions

1 Vocabulary Positive and negative descriptions

A 🎧 **Make the words negative. Write them in the chart. Then listen and check your answers.**

convenient	creative	eventful	significant
conventional	effective	imaginative	successful

un-	in-

B **PAIR WORK** **What do you think? Discuss the sentences. Circle the correct word.**

1 The first computers were huge. They filled an entire room. They were very **convenient** / **inconvenient** for everyday use.

2 Coco Chanel's fashion designs are world famous. They were so **imaginative** / **unimaginative**. Many people have copied them.

3 The new hybrid car is **conventional** / **unconventional**. I've never seen one like it. It uses air, not gasoline.

4 One day in 1847, Joseph Fry discovered a way to make chocolate bars. What an **eventful** / **uneventful** day that was! What would we do without them?

2 Language in context Early inventions

A 🎧 **Read the descriptions of early inventions. What was each invention used for?**

The abacus is over 5,000 years old. It was used to count numbers. It was such an effective tool in China and the Middle East that it spread to other parts of the world and is still used in many countries today.

Rubber was first used by the ancient Mayans in Mexico and Central America about 3,500 years ago. They took rubber from trees, boiled it, and made rubber balls, which they used in ancient ball games.

More than 2,000 years ago, the ancient Romans built aqueducts to bring water into their cities from miles away. Some of these aqueducts were so well made that they still carry water today.

B **What are some modern examples of these inventions? Do you know any other early inventions?**

3 Grammar 🎧 So and *such*

> *Use* so *and* such *with an adjective to make the adjective*
>
> | so + adjective | such + a / an + adjective + singular noun |
> |---|---|
> | It was **so creative**. | It was **such a creative** idea. |
> | It was **so well made**. | It was **such a well-made** aqueduct. |
>
> *Use a* that *clause with* so *or* such *to show a result.*
> The abacus was **so** effective **that** it spread to other places.
> The abacus was **such** an effective tool **that** it spread to other places.

A Complete the sentences with *so* or *such*. Then compare with a partner.

1   The wheel was _____ a significant invention.

2   Her ideas were _____ unimaginative.

3   His inventions have been _____ successful.

4   His thinking is _____ unconventional.

5   She was _____ a creative woman.

6   Wireless Internet access is _____ convenient.

B Complete the sentences. Use *so . . . that* or *such . . . that*. Then compare with a partner.

1   Online streaming is _____ (popular) cable TV subscriptions have decreased.

2   I think the Perfect Cake Cutter was _____ (an ineffective invention) no one wanted to buy it.

3   Smartphones are _____ (inexpensive) almost everyone has one.

4   MP3 players were _____ (a big success) they changed the way we listen to music.

4 Pronunciation Emphatic stress

A 🎧 Listen and repeat. Notice the extra stress on *so* and *such* for emphasis.

That is **so** conventional.   That is **such** a conventional thing to say.

B PAIR WORK Practice the sentences in Exercise 3A. Pay attention to your pronunciation of *so* and *such*.

5 Speaking Top inventions

GROUP WORK Discuss three important inventions in each category. Why are they so important?

communication	technology	transportation

6 Keep talking!

Go to page 137 for more practice.

I can describe important inventions. ✓

B Got any suggestions?

Interactions Solutions

A Look at the picture in Part B. What problem do the people have? How can they solve it?

B 🎧 Listen to the conversation. How do they plan to solve the problem? Then practice the conversation.

Ralph	Here we go . . . almost there.
Carl	This sofa is going to look great in my living room. Thanks again for helping me.
Jim	No problem.
Ralph	Wait a minute. It doesn't fit.
Carl	What? Are you kidding?
Jim	Did you measure it before you bought it?
Carl	Of course. There should be enough room. I even made a sketch, see?
Ralph	Well, I'm sure there's something we can do. Do you have any ideas?
Jim	Well, one idea could be to turn the sofa the other way.
Carl	It's worth a try. If that doesn't work, I'm not sure what else to do.

C 🎧 Read the expressions below. Complete each box with a similar expression from the conversation. Then listen and check your answers.

Eliciting an idea

_____

- Got any ideas?
- Got any suggestions?

Suggesting a solution

_____

- Something we could try is to . . .
- One solution might be to . . .

D **GROUP WORK** Have conversations like the one in Part B. Use these ideas.

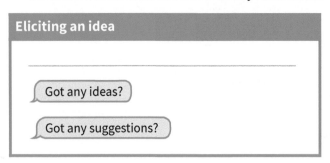
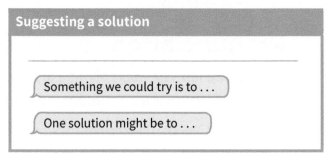

go through the window   remove the legs

2 Listening Sticky situations

A Look at the pictures. What problems do you see?

B 🎧 Listen to people discuss how to solve the problems in Part A. Number the pictures in Part A from 1 to 4.

C 🎧 Listen again. Check (✓) the solution they decide to try.

1. ☐ Stand on the reef and lift the boat.
   ☐ Wait and let the tide lift the boat.

2. ☐ Take the parrot's cage outside.
   ☐ Give the parrot treats.

3. ☐ Pour oil around the opening.
   ☐ Put the jar under hot running water.

4. ☐ Add weight to push the truck down.
   ☐ Remove all the air from the tires.

3 Speaking Inventive solutions

A `GROUP WORK` What could you do in these situations? Discuss your answers.

1. You forgot your wallet and have no money to pay for the dinner you have just eaten at a restaurant.

2. Your pet cat is sitting at the end of a high tree branch. It's so scared that it won't come down.

3. You realize you made plans with your best friend and your mother for the same night.

4. You discover you locked your keys inside your apartment.

A: Do you have any ideas about situation 1?

B: Well, one idea could be to call a friend for help.

C: Or one solution might be to wash the dishes to pay for your meal.

B `CLASS ACTIVITY` Share your solutions. Vote on the best solution for each situation.

I can elicit ideas. ✓
I can suggest solutions. ✓

C Accidental inventions

1 Vocabulary Verb and noun formation

A 🎧 Read about the inventions. Complete the chart with the missing form of words. Then listen and check your answers.

Sometimes a successful **invention** happens by accident: the tea bag, for example. Thomas Sullivan **introduced** tea bags to the world in 1908. He was a New York tea importer. He sent tea to his clients in tin cans. But tin was so heavy and expensive that he needed a more convenient way to send it. So he **designed** inexpensive bags to hold the tea leaves and sent them instead. Thomas's customers were supposed to open the bags and put the leaves in hot water. Instead, they used the entire bag. But this **innovation** worked! Immediately, tea bags **proved** to be a big **success**.

Ruth Wakefield **created** another accidental invention in her Massachusetts hotel in 1930. One day, Ruth didn't have enough chocolate for her usual chocolate cookie recipe. So she cut a chocolate bar into small pieces and made more cookies with less chocolate. The chocolate chips didn't melt completely, but her guests loved them! Ruth **developed** the original chocolate chip cookie. And her recipe has never needed much **improvement**. It's still the world's most popular chocolate chip cookie recipe today.

Verb	Noun
invented	**invention**
	introduction
	design

Verb	Noun
innovated	
	proof
succeeded	

Verb	Noun
	creation
	development
improved	

B PAIR WORK Choose four of the words from the chart. Make sentences with these words about something you have done. Tell your partner.

2 Conversation A delicious discovery

A 🎧 Listen to the conversation. Why did the chef get angry?

Dana   Do you know how the potato chip was invented?

Emma   I have no idea.

Dana   Apparently, in 1853, a customer in a restaurant sent his French fries back to the kitchen several times because they weren't thin enough. The chef was so angry that he sliced them even thinner, fried them again, and sent them back to the customer.

Emma   And the customer liked them?

Dana   Yeah, he asked for more! The chef's creation was such a success that they were requested by other customers, too. At that time they were only salted, but since then, lots of different flavors have been developed.

Emma   Fascinating. So, can I have my chips back?

B 🎧 Listen to the rest of the conversation. What three countries do they mention? What flavors of potato chips are mentioned for each country?

3 Grammar 🎧 The passive

Active	Passive
Simple present: People still **use** her recipe today.	Her recipe **is** still **used** today.
Simple past: A chef **invented** it in 1853.	It **was invented** in 1853.
Present perfect: Companies **have developed** many flavors since 1853.	Many flavors **have been developed** since 1853.

A Rewrite these sentences. Use the passive voice. Then compare with a partner.

1 Thomas Sullivan introduced tea bags to the world in 1908.
Tea bags were introduced to the world in 1908.

2 Sullivan designed small bags to hold the tea.

_____

3 A man produced the first flavored potato chip in the 1950s.

_____

4 Potato chip makers have developed many unique flavors.

_____

B Complete the sentences. Use the passive voice with the simple present, simple past, or present perfect form. Then compare with a partner.

The 3M company _____ (know) for its innovation for a long time. But there have been mistakes along the way. Today, employees _____ (encourage) to learn from past mistakes. That's how Arthur Fry learned about a special glue. It _____ (create) in the 3M lab in 1968. The glue wasn't strong enough, so it _____ (forget). But Fry found it in 1974 and used it to develop Post-it Notes. The original Post-it Notes _____ (improve) since then, and now they _____ (sell) all over the world.

4 Speaking Early innovations

GROUP WORK Look at these products. What improvements have been made to the products recently? Have all of the improvements been good ones?

"Tennis shoes have been made lighter. Their design has been improved a lot."

5 Keep talking!

Go to page 138 for more practice.

I can discuss how things have been improved. ✅

D Making life easier

1 Reading 🎧

A Look at the picture. What do you think this article is about?

B Read the article. Check (✓) the best title.
- ☐ Top Innovations in Japan
- ☐ The Future of Technology
- ☐ Technology Helps Japan's Elderly
- ☐ Growing Old in Japan

ONCE UPON A TIME,

there was a land where robotic bears helped lift the elderly out of bed and into wheelchairs. In this land, robotic seals comforted lonely people and were an **essential** part of elder care.

Is this science fiction? Not in Japan. These robots already exist, and you may actually experience them as you get older. These examples of **state-of-the-art** technology are helping to solve a big problem for the Japanese – the problem of taking care of their **senior citizens**.

It is estimated that 40% of the population in Japan will be over 65 by 2055. At the same time, there will be an estimated 16% decrease in the size of the workforce by 2030. This **shortage** of labor presents a serious challenge:

Who will look after all the people in their **golden years**? There are simply not enough younger people to care for this older population. And with the breakdown of traditional family responsibilities, a growing number of elderly are living away from their families and the family care they have been given in the past.

Robots to the rescue! Robotic beds that are controlled by voice can change from a bed to a wheelchair on command. The robotic bear nurse can lift patients who weigh up to 135 pounds (61 kilos). And for comfort and friendship, a soft robotic pet seal has been designed to show emotions with facial expressions, movement, and noises, and to respond to touch. These are just a few of the inventions that are so promising. Robots are the future of elder care.

C Find the words in **bold** in the article. Circle the correct meanings.

1	**essential**	a. necessary	b. unnatural
2	**state-of-the-art**	a. the most advanced	b. imaginary
3	**senior citizens**	a. elderly people	b. people who need help
4	**shortage**	a. too much of	b. not enough of
5	**golden years**	a. time before retirement	b. time after retirement

D CLASS ACTIVITY What is your opinion of using robots and technology to help the elderly? What are some other ways that robots and technology are helping people? Discuss your ideas.

2 **Listening** A robot pet?

A 🎧 Listen to a commercial for i-Cybie, a robot dog. Check (✓) the things the i-Cybie can do.

- ☐ eat
- ☐ sing
- ☐ play
- ☐ sit
- ☐ scratch its ear
- ☐ dance
- ☐ taste
- ☐ smell
- ☐ show emotion
- ☐ sleep
- ☐ respond to commands
- ☐ do a yoga position

B 🎧 Listen to Jason tell his friend Tina about his new i-Cybie. Write two things he likes and two things he doesn't like about his new pet.

What he likes	What he doesn't like
1 _____	1 _____
2 _____	2 _____

3 **Writing and speaking** An invention

A GROUP WORK Brainstorm inventions that would make your life easier. Make a list.

B Choose one of the inventions. Draw a picture of it. Then write a paragraph about it. Give it a name, explain who it's for, and discuss what it does.

Charger Baseball Cap
The Charger Baseball Cap is for anyone who loves laying out in the sun, but doesn't want to worry about their phone battery. The front of the cap has a solar charging panel that wirelessly charges your cell phone. It looks like a stylish baseball cap, but . . .

C CLASS ACTIVITY Walk around the class. Show the picture of your invention to five people. Describe it and try to convince your classmates that they need your invention.

"You have to get a Charger Baseball Cap. You can charge your phone battery while you're outside, but you also . . ."

D As a class, vote on and give these awards for the best inventions.

the best overall invention	the most innovative invention
the greatest improvement to people's lives	the most useful invention

I can describe something I invented. ✓

Wrap-up

1 Quick pair review

Lesson A Test your partner!

Say a positive descriptive adjective. Can your partner write the negative adjective correctly? Take turns. You and your partner have one minute.

"Conventional."

1 _unconventional_   3 _____   5 _____

2 _____   4 _____   6 _____

Lesson B Give your opinion!

What are solutions to these problems? Elicit ideas and suggest solutions. Take turns. You and your partner have two minutes.

- You have only one day to study for a test.
- You can't find your keys.
- You have a broken-down car and need to get to work.
- You have to fit a big piano through a small door.

A: I have only one day to study for a test. Got any suggestions?

B: One idea could be to stay up all night and study.

Lesson C Do you remember?

Write A for active and P for passive. You have one minute.

1 The Internet was invented in the 1970s. _____

2 My mother doesn't like new technology. _____

3 This cell phone has won an award for best design. _____

4 That movie has been seen all over the world. _____

Lesson D Guess!

Describe an invention, but don't say its name. Can your partner guess what it is? You and your partner have two minutes.

A: This invention is so useful. It helps you see.

B: Glasses?

A: No. It goes in a lamp.

2 In the real world

What's a great invention? Find information online about one of these inventions, or choose your own idea. Then write about it.

| computer mouse | pencil sharpener | Silly Putty | TV remote control |

- What is it?
- Who invented it?
- When was it invented?
- What do you think about the invention?

Silly Putty

Silly Putty is a toy for children. It was invented by James Wright in the 1940s.

8 Lessons in life

LESSON A
- Prefixes: *mis-*, *dis-*, and *re-*
- Past perfect

LESSON B
- Expressing worry
- Reassuring someone

LESSON C
- Expressions with *make* and *get*
- Third conditional

LESSON D
- Reading: "Tuesday, January 9, 2007"
- Writing: About a memorable day

Warm Up

A Describe the pictures. What's happening? How do you think each person feels?

B What would you do if these things happened to you?

A Why did I do that?

1 Vocabulary Prefixes: *mis-*, *dis-*, and *re-*

A 🎧 Read the sentences. Match the prefixes *mis-*, *dis-*, and *re-* and their meanings.

1 I **mis**spelled your name. Can you correct it?   _____   a. do something again

2 Please **dis**regard my email. It wasn't important.   _____   b. do something wrong

3 Let's **re**consider. There might be a better way.   _____   c. don't do something

B 🎧 Add the correct prefixes to the words, and write them in the chart. Then listen and check your answers.

agree	continue	judge	make	regard	think
consider	do	like	pronounce	spell	understand

mis-	dis-	re-
_____ _____	_____ _____	_____ _____
_____ _____	_____ _____	_____ _____

C PAIR WORK Answer the questions.

● What word do you often misspell? What word do you often mispronounce?

● Do you ever disagree with your friends? Do you disregard their advice? Why?

2 Language in context Awkward situations

A 🎧 Listen to two people describe awkward situations. What was awkward about each situation?

When I was emailing my classmate about a surprise party for my friend Leo, I hit "send" and it went to Leo. I'd sent the email to Leo before I realized my mistake. I called him and asked him to disregard the email. Luckily, he hadn't read it yet.

— *John*

The other day, my boss mispronounced my name in the elevator. He had done it once before, and I hadn't corrected him. But this time, I reconsidered. Unfortunately, by the time I started to say something, my boss had already left the elevator.

— *Angelica*

B What do you think? Did John and Angelica do the right thing? Has anything similar ever happened to you?

3 Grammar 🎧 Past perfect

Use the past perfect to describe an action that took place before another action in the past.
I**'d sent** the email to Leo before I realized my mistake.

The words yet and already are often used with the past perfect.
I asked him to disregard the message. Luckily, **he hadn't** read it yet.
By the time I started to say something, my boss **had** already **left**.

Contraction   I**'d** = I **had**

**Complete the sentences. Use the simple past and past perfect in each sentence.
Then compare with a partner.**

1   I _____ (plan) on working all weekend, but then
    I _____ (reconsider) and went to the beach instead.

2   I was so late this morning. By the time I _____ (get) to work,
    I _____ (miss) the whole meeting.

3   Alice _____ (wake up) at 9:30 because she _____
    (forget) to set her alarm clock for 8:00.

4   Before Richard and Alex _____ (meet),
    they _____ (be) e-pals for a year.

5   I _____ (call) my friend to cancel our plans.
    Luckily, he _____ (not / leave) yet.

4 Pronunciation Reduction of *had*

A 🎧 **Listen and repeat. Notice how *had* is pronounced /d/ in the past perfect.**

I**'d** sent the email to Leo.   My boss **had** already left the elevator.

B PAIR WORK **Practice the sentences in Exercise 3. Pay attention to your pronunciation
of the past perfect.**

5 Speaking I'd forgotten to . . .

A **Choose a situation and prepare to talk about it. Think about the events that
happened *before* and *after*.**

you disagreed with someone	you misjudged someone	you redid something incorrectly
you forgot something	you misunderstood someone	you were very late

B GROUP WORK **Tell your classmates what happened. Answer any questions.**

A: I was embarrassed at a job interview once. I'd forgotten to turn off my cell phone.

B: Really? Did the job interviewer say anything?

6 Keep talking!

Go to page 139 for more practice.

I can describe events in the past.   75

3 I'm sure you'll do fine.

1 Interactions Worries and reassurance

A In which of these situations do you feel the most confident? The least confident?

public speaking in English	speaking in front of a large group
public speaking in your own language	speaking in front of a small group

B 🎧 Listen to the conversation. What is Feng worried about? Then practice the conversation.

Mei   Hi, Feng. How are you?

Feng   Oh, hi, Mei. I'm fine, I guess. But I have to give a presentation in my English class, and I'm kind of worried about it.

Mei   Really? Why?

Feng   Well, I always forget what I'm planning to say. I'm not confident speaking in front of people.

Mei   Can you use notes?

Feng   Yeah, I can, so that will help.

Mei   I'm sure you'll do fine. You're great in front of people.

Feng   Do you really think so?

Mei   I do. Just try to relax.

Feng   Well, thanks. We'll see how it goes.

C 🎧 Read the expressions below. Complete each box with a similar expression from the conversation. Then listen and check your answers.

Expressing worry	Reassuring someone
_____	_____
I'm a little anxious about it.	I'm sure you'll be OK.
I'm pretty nervous about it.	Don't worry. Everything will work out.

D **PAIR WORK** Number the sentences from 1 to 6. Then practice with a partner.

_____ A When is it?

___1___ A Hi, Bill. How are you?

_____ A This weekend? Well, I'm sure you'll do OK.

_____ B Really? I'm not so sure. But thanks anyway.

_____ B It's this weekend.

_____ B Fine, I guess. But I'm pretty nervous about my driver's test.

2 Listening Feeling anxious

A 🎧 **Listen to four friends talk about situations that worry them. Number the pictures from 1 to 4.**

B 🎧 **Listen again. What do their friends say to reassure them? Write the sentences.**

1 _____

2 _____

3 _____

4 _____

3 Speaking Please don't worry.

A PAIR WORK **Role-play the situation.**

Student A: You have been invited to a party. You are a little anxious about it. You're afraid you won't know anyone. Tell Student B how you feel.

Student B: Student A is a little anxious about going to a party. Find out why. Reassure your friend.

A: I'm pretty nervous about going to this party.

B: Why are you so nervous?

A: I won't know anyone there.

B: But you can meet new people there. Don't worry. . . .

B Change roles and role-play the situation.

Student A: You are changing schools. You are worried about it. You're afraid you might not make new friends easily. Tell Student B how you feel.

Student B: Student A is changing schools and is worried about it. Find out why. Reassure your friend.

C PAIR WORK **Write a role play about reassuring someone in a difficult situation. Give it to another pair to role-play. Use one of these situations, or use your own ideas.**

| doing a home-stay abroad | getting a new roommate | traveling alone |

I can express worry. ✓

I can reassure someone. ✓

77

C What if...?

1 Vocabulary Expressions with *make* and *get*

A 🎧 Match the statements. Then listen and check your answers.

1. I hate to **make a fool of myself.** _____
2. I always **make an effort** to do my best in school. _____
3. I often **make mistakes.** _____
4. I never **make a big deal** about my birthday. _____
5. I **make up my mind** easily. _____
6. I never **get into trouble.** _____
7. If someone isn't nice to me, I try to **get over it** quickly. _____
8. I always try to **get out of** doing the dishes. _____
9. My friends sometimes **get on my nerves.** _____
10. I like to **get rid of** things I don't need. _____

a. I sometimes don't even tell anyone.
b. I dislike it when people laugh at my mistakes.
c. I try very hard.
d. I am careless.
e. It's not difficult for me to decide things.
f. I just disregard it.
g. I always try to follow the rules.
h. I get annoyed when they play loud music.
i. It's my least favorite chore.
j. I don't like to keep unnecessary things.

B PAIR WORK Which statements in Part A are true for you?
Discuss your answers.

"I like to get rid of old newspapers and magazines, but my roommate likes to save them."

2 Conversation A new boyfriend

A 🎧 Listen to the conversation. What mistake did Alicia make?

Dan So, how was Aki's party?

Alicia Well, the party was fun. But I'd forgotten it was her birthday, so I was a little embarrassed.

Dan Why?

Alicia I didn't bring a gift. If I'd remembered, I'd have brought her something really nice.

Dan Well, I'm sure she didn't mind.

Alicia Then, I think I made a fool of myself at the party. We all had to sing, and you know how bad my voice is.

Dan Oh, come on.

Alicia I tried to get out of it, but I couldn't. And that's when I met Santiago. Just think. If I hadn't sung at the party, I wouldn't have met Santiago.

Dan Santiago? Who's Santiago?

Alicia He's my new boyfriend.

B 🎧 Listen to the rest of the conversation. What's Santiago like?
What gets on Alicia's nerves?

78

3 Grammar 🎧 Third conditional

> *Third conditional sentences describe hypothetical situations in the past.*
> *Use the past perfect in the* if *clause and* would have + *past participle in the main clause.*
>   If I**'d remembered**, I **would have brought** her something.
>   If I **hadn't forgotten**, I **would have brought** her a gift.
>   If she **had missed** the party, she **wouldn't have met** Santiago.
>   If she **hadn't gone** to the party, she **wouldn't have met** him.
> *Remember*: I**'d** = I **would** *or* I **had**

A Read the conditional sentences. Circle the true statements about them.

1 If Henry had made an effort, he would have passed all of his exams.

  a. Henry made an effort.　　　　b. Henry didn't make an effort.

2 If Mike had followed the instructions, he wouldn't have made a mistake.

  a. Mike made a mistake.　　　　b. Mike didn't make a mistake.

3 If Luz hadn't become a doctor, she would have become an artist.

  a. Luz became a doctor.　　　　b. Luz didn't become a doctor.

4 If Andrea hadn't sold her old books online, she wouldn't have gotten rid of them.

  a. Andrea got rid of her books.　　　　b. Andrea didn't get rid of her books.

B Complete the sentences with the third conditional.
Then compare with a partner.

1 If I _____ (know) about the party,
　I _____ (not / make) such a fool of myself.

2 If you _____ (come) home before midnight,
　you _____ (not / get) into trouble.

3 If I _____ (not / get) rid of my old cell phone,
　I _____ (let) you have it.

4 I _____ (make) up my mind easily if
　I _____ (not / have) so many choices.

4 Speaking If only I hadn't . . .

A Check (✓) the things you've done.

☐ made a mistake　　　　☐ gotten rid of something important

☐ made an effort to do something　　　　☐ gotten out of something

☐ made a fool of yourself　　　　☐ gotten into trouble

B PAIR WORK Tell your partner the things you checked in Part A. What would have been different if you hadn't done these things? Share your stories.

5 Keep talking!

Go to page 140 for more practice.

I can talk about how things might have been. ✓

D A day to remember

1 Reading 🎧

A The great hockey player Wayne Gretzky once said: "I skate to where the puck is going to be, not where it has been." Why do you think Steve Jobs liked this quote so much?

Tuesday, January 9, 2007

STEVE JOBS

co-Founder and CEO of Apple, was about to walk onto a stage in San Francisco. Moments before, he had gathered his team together and told them to remember this moment, because in the next hour, everything would change.

Jobs was about to unveil the iPhone, which would become one of the most popular products of all time.

The team was more than a little nervous about the event. When they had arrived that day, the iPhone didn't actually work yet. It would often crash when trying to play a song or run an app. But the company had been working to remake the mobile phone for 2 ½ years, and Jobs made up his mind it was time to introduce the iPhone to the world. The engineers had prepared a presentation with features they thought could work, but they were terrified they might have made some mistakes.

It wasn't the first time that Apple had launched a revolutionary product. When Apple introduced the Macintosh computer in 1984, it changed personal computing forever. And when the company launched the first iPod music player in 2001, it revolutionized the way we listen to music – and the way music is sold.

Despite the pressure, Jobs was calm. He was used to speaking in front of a large group. After he had taken the stage, he told the crowd he actually had three revolutionary new products to show them – a touchscreen iPod, a mobile phone, and an Internet device. "Are you getting it?" he asked. "This is one device. And we are calling it iPhone."

If the presentation had failed, it would have been a disaster. But everything went perfectly. Jobs showed the crowd of 4,000 how you could easily switch from surfing the Internet to making a call to listening to music. He demonstrated how you could use your fingers to zoom in on a photo, and how Apple had gotten rid of the physical keyboard with buttons that was common on other phones. And he showed how the iPhone put the Internet in your pocket for the first time, letting you check your email or surf the Web from anywhere.

A number of other products had included some of these features, but the iPhone was the first to combine them all – and a lot more. When Jobs had finished his presentation, mobile phones would never be the same again.

B Read the excerpt again. Number the events from 1 to 8.

_____ Jobs told his team to remember this moment.

_____ Jobs took the stage.

_____ The Apple team prepared a presentation.

_____ Jobs made up his mind to unveil the iPhone.

_____ Jobs demonstrated the iPhone's features.

_____ Apple launched the iPod.

_____ The Apple team developed the iPhone.

___1___ Apple introduced the Mac computer.

C Do you remember a time before the iPhone? What do you imagine that mobile phones were like at that time? How do you think people surfed the Internet, took pictures, listened to music, and followed maps before the iPhone?

2 **Listening** Looking back

A 🎧 Listen to four people talk about important days in their lives.
Check (✓) which day they're talking about.

	Day	What made it a memorable day?
1	☐ first day of middle school ☐ first day of high school	☐ Her friend was a teacher at the school. ☐ Her friend was going to the same school.
2	☐ wedding day ☐ birth of a child	☐ Their parents were there. ☐ The announcement appeared in the newspaper.
3	☐ first day at work ☐ last day at work	☐ His co-workers gave him a party. ☐ He'd traveled on his own in Europe.
4	☐ first airplane trip ☐ first trip over seas	☐ She could speak Korean with her host family. ☐ Her hosts were so kind and friendly.

B 🎧 Listen again. Check (✓) what made the day memorable.

3 **Writing and speaking** About a memorable day

A Think about a memorable day. Use these ideas or your own ideas.

the day you got accepted to college	your first airplane ride
the day you spoke English to a native speaker	your first day at a new job
the first time you rode a bicycle	your first day of school
a special celebration	

B Write a paragraph about your memorable day. Use the questions and the model
paragraph to help you.

- When was it?
- What made the day memorable?
- Did you look forward to this day?
- What did you do that day?
- How did you feel then?

> **A Memorable Day**
> One of the best days of my life was when
> I got accepted to City University.
> I had always wanted to go there. I'd been
> pretty worried until I got my official
> acceptance letter. I remember I called
> some of my friends to tell them. Then
> that night, I went out with my family to
> celebrate. I was so happy that day.

C GROUP WORK Share your writing. Ask and answer questions about that day.
As a group, decide which day was the most interesting, unusual, or exciting day.

I can describe a memorable day. ☑

Wrap-up

1 Quick pair review

Lesson A Do you remember?

Cross out the words that don't belong. You have one minute.

1 *mis-*   spell   understand   ~~think~~   pronounce   judge
2 *re-*   do   think   consider   make   agree
3 *dis-*   agree   make   continue   regard   like

Lesson B Brainstorm!

Make a list of ways to express worry and ways to reassure someone.
How many do you remember? You have two minutes.

Lesson C Give your opinion!

Imagine these things happened to you. Ask your partner what he or she
would have done. Take turns. You and your partner have two minutes.

- You forgot to take your passport to the airport.
- You didn't remember a friend's birthday.
- You didn't go to class on the day of a test.

A: What would you have done if you had forgotten your passport?

B: If I had forgotten my passport, I would have called my friend and asked her
to bring it to me. What about you?

Lesson D Guess!

Think about important first days in a person's life. Guess how old your partner
was for each of these firsts. You and your partner have two minutes.

first time he or she traveled alone	first time he or she spoke English
first time he or she rode a bicycle	(your own idea)

A: Were you 18 the first time you traveled alone?

B: No, I was younger.

2 In the real world

What was the first day of school like for someone in your family or for a close friend?
Interview the person. Then write about it.

First Day of School

My father was nervous on his first day of school. His father,
my grandfather, took him to school. My father met Charlie
on the first day of school. Charlie became his best friend.

9 Can you believe it?

LESSON A
- Suffixes: *-ful* and *-less*
- Past modals for speculating

LESSON B
- Expressing probability
- Expressing improbability

LESSON C
- Mysterious events
- Embedded questions

LESSON D
- Reading: "The Woman Who Can't Forget"
- Writing: A story

Warm Up

A Describe the pictures. What do you see?

B Can you explain the pictures? Think of several possible explanations.

A Everyday explanations

1 Vocabulary Suffixes: -ful and -less

A 🎧 Circle the correct words to complete the sentences. Then listen and check your answers.

1 I can't get this old computer to work at all. It's **useful** / **useless** for me to even try.

2 The storm was so **powerful** / **powerless** that it destroyed a hundred homes.

3 I read about a man who raised a lion as his pet. He was totally **fearful** / **fearless**.

4 The police made people leave the building because the bad odor was **harmful** / **harmless** to their health.

5 Jane was fined $300 for **careful** / **careless** driving.

6 I couldn't understand his explanations at all. They were so **meaningful** / **meaningless**.

7 Sara gave me a lovely graduation present. That was very **thoughtful** / **thoughtless** of her.

8 I'm **hopeful** / **hopeless** that I'll get a good grade on my exam. I have been studying a lot.

B PAIR WORK Make sentences about your experiences. Use the words you did *not* circle in Part A. Tell your partner.

2 Language in context Explainable behavior

A 🎧 Read the online chat between co-workers. Why are they talking about Kenny?

< Online Chat   **— ✕**

Maria, Ethan, James...

Maria: Ethan, did you see Kenny yesterday?

Ethan: How could I miss him? He was wearing a suit. He looked so impressive in his suit and tie! ☺.

Maria: Yeah, I know. But it was really hot yesterday, so he couldn't have been comfortable in a suit.

Ethan: Did you ask him why he was so dressed up?

Maria: Yeah, but it was useless. He wouldn't say a word.

Ethan: He might have had a presentation to give.

Maria: Yeah, that's possible. Or maybe it wasn't meaningful at all. He could have simply felt like dressing up in a suit.

James: Hi, you guys. Did you hear about Kenny?

Ethan: Actually, we were just chatting about him.

James: Well, he called me earlier today. He said he had interviewed for a new job yesterday. And they offered it to him!

Maria: That explains it! He must have gone to his interview after work. He wasn't very careful about it, was he?

Write a Message...   Send

B What are some other reasons that people dress up for work?

3 Grammar ∩ Past modals for speculating

Speculating with more certainty
> He **must have gone** to his interview.
> It was really hot yesterday, so he **couldn't have been** comfortable in a suit.

Speculating with less certainty
> He **might have had** a presentation.
> He **could have felt** like dressing up.

A Complete the conversations with past modals. Then practice with a partner.

1 A Why hasn't Kate been answering her phone?

  B Who knows? She could _____ (turn) off the ringer.

2 A Why did Randy quit his job yesterday?

  B I'm not sure. He might _____ (get) a better one.

3 A Have you seen Nancy?

  B No, she hasn't come to work yet. She could _____ (oversleep) again.

4 A Is Emma here? She's late for her appointment. That never happens.

  B Something important must _____ (delay) her.

5 A What's wrong? Did Jack forget your birthday?

  B He could _____ (not/forget) it. He always remembers.

B Read the questions in Part A. Write different explanations. Then practice with a partner.

1 _____

2 _____

3 _____

4 _____

5 _____

4 Speaking Possible explanations

GROUP WORK Discuss possible explanations for these situations.

1 Your classmate seemed very forgetful today.

2 Your friend is fluent in Russian after only
three months of study.

3 Your friend used to be very careless,
but suddenly you can depend on her for anything.

4 Your cousin used to be afraid of animals,
but now he is fearless.

"My classmate might have had very little sleep. That could have made him forgetful."

5 Keep talking!

Students A and B go to page 141 and Students C and D go to page 142 for more practice.

I can speculate about everyday situations. ✓

B I'm pretty sure that . . .

1 **Interactions** Probability and improbability

A **PAIR WORK** **Try this experiment. Do it ten times, then change roles.**

Student A: Think of a number between 1 and 10.

Student B: Try to read your partner's mind by guessing if the number is *even* (2, 4, 6, . . .) or *odd* (1, 3, 5, . . .).

Did you guess correctly? Who else in the class guessed correctly? How many times?

B 🎧 **Listen to the conversation. How does Daniela explain mind-reading between twins? Then practice the conversation.**

Daniela	I saw a TV show yesterday about twins who read each other's minds. Do you think that's possible?
Jenny	Well, twins spend a lot of time together. It's likely that they can read each other's thoughts.
Daniela	Really?
Jenny	Why not? When they're young, some twins develop a secret language only they understand. That shows that twins can be special.
Daniela	But I doubt that anyone can really read minds. They could have guessed each other's thoughts because they spend a lot of time together. But that's not mind reading.
Jenny	You are so skeptical.
Daniela	I know. So, should we order now?
Jenny	You just read my mind!

C 🎧 **Read the expressions below. Complete each box with a similar expression from the conversation. Then listen and check your answers.**

Expressing probability	**Expressing improbability**
_____	_____
I'm pretty sure that . . .	It's doubtful that . . .
It's very probable that . . .	It's highly unlikely that . . .

D **GROUP WORK** **Check (✓) the sentences you think are probable. Then talk to your group about what is probable and what is improbable.**

☐ Twins have a special relationship.   ☐ Twins are more alike than different.

☐ Only some people can read minds.   ☐ All twins can read each other's minds.

2 Listening Likely . . . or unlikely?

A **PAIR WORK** Which of these things can help you know what others are thinking?

body language	emotions	hairstyles	memory
dreams	facial expressions	laughing	tone of voice

B 🎧 Listen to Karl tell his friend Jenna about an article on mind-reading. How do people read minds? Look at Part A again, and circle the ways that are mentioned in the article.

C 🎧 Listen to the rest of the conversation. Correct the statements.

1 Strangers can read each other's minds ~~30%~~ 20% of the time.

2 Married couples can read each other's minds 45% of the time.

3 No one can read minds more than 6% of the time.

4 There's a big difference in how well men and women can read minds.

5 It's likely that Jenna believes what Karl says about men and women.

3 Speaking Anything's possible.

A Read the statements. Do you think they are probable? Write P (probable) or I (improbable) next to each statement.

_____ People will travel through time someday.

_____ Some people can remember their past lives.

_____ Some people can predict the weather.

_____ Some people can communicate with animals.

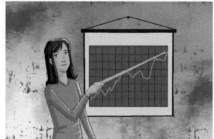
_____ Some people can predict trends in the stock market.

_____ Some people can heal themselves with their mind.

B **GROUP WORK** Share your ideas.

A: I doubt that people will travel through time someday.

B: I agree. It's highly unlikely.

C: I'm not so sure. I bet it will happen someday because . . .

I can express probability and improbability. ✓

87

C History's mysteries

1 Vocabulary Mysterious events

A 🎧 **Match the words and the stories. Then listen and check your answers.**

a	abduction
b	disappearance
c	discovery
d	escape
e	explosion
f	theft

1 _____ In 1962, three men broke out of San Francisco's Alcatraz prison. They were never seen again.

2 _____ In 1908, a huge object from space exploded over Siberia. It destroyed 80 million trees.

3 _____ In 1937, Amelia Earhart disappeared during a flight over the Pacific Ocean. She was never seen again.

4 _____ In 1961, Betty and Barney Hill claimed they were taken aboard a UFO by unfriendly aliens.

5 _____ In 1985, divers found large rocks near Japan that some believe are a lost underwater city.

6 _____ In 1990, robbers in Boston stole paintings worth $300 million. They have never been recovered.

B PAIR WORK **Choose three words from Part A. What are other examples of these types of events? Tell your partner.**

2 Conversation It remains a mystery.

A 🎧 **Listen to the conversation. What does the tourist learn about the Great Pyramid?**

Guide   No one really knows how the Egyptian pyramids were built. There are many theories and new discoveries, but it remains a mystery.

Tourist   Do you have any idea how long it took to build them?

Guide   Yes. It took about 20 years to build the tallest one, the Great Pyramid.

Tourist   Can you tell me how tall it is?

Guide   It's more than 450 feet, or about 139 meters. It was the tallest structure in the world for thousands of years.

Tourist   Really?

Guide   Yes. It was the world's tallest structure until the Eiffel Tower was built.

Tourist   That's amazing! Do you know how many pyramids were built in Egypt?

Guide   No one knows. But at least 80 pyramids have survived, and many more are still under the sand.

B 🎧 **Listen to the rest of the conversation. Why was the Sphinx built? What happened to its nose?**

3 Grammar 🎧 Embedded questions

An embedded question is a question included in another question.

Wh- questions	Embedded Wh- questions
How many pyramids were built?	Do you know **how many pyramids were built?**
How long did it take to build?	Do you have any idea **how long it took to build?**
How tall is the Great Pyramid?	Can you tell me **how tall the Great Pyramid is?**
Yes / no questions	**Embedded yes / no questions**
Was the Sphinx painted?	Do you know **if the Sphinx was painted?**
Are there any chambers?	Can you tell me **if there are any chambers?**
Did its nose fall off?	Do you know **if its nose fell off?**

Rewrite the questions. Use embedded questions. Then compare with a partner.

1 Have there been many thefts from the pyramids?

  A Do you know _____?   B Yes, many.

2 How long was the Great Pyramid the world's tallest structure?

  A Do you know _____?   B For 3,800 years.

3 How many chambers are there in the Great Pyramid?

  A Can you tell me _____?   B There are three.

4 Can tourists climb the Sphinx?

  A Do you have any idea _____?   B No, it's not allowed.

5 Did aliens build the pyramids?

  A Do you know _____?   B It's highly unlikely.

4 Pronunciation Intonation in embedded questions

A 🎧 Listen and repeat. Notice the falling intonation in embedded questions.

Can you tell me how tall it is?   Do you know if the Sphinx was painted?

B PAIR WORK Practice the embedded questions in Exercise 3. Pay attention to your intonation.

5 Speaking Endless possibilities

PAIR WORK Discuss possible explanations for the mysteries in Exercise 1.

A: Do you have and idea what happened to Amelia Earhart?

B: No one does. But she might have crashed on an island.

6 Keep talking!

Go to page 143 for more practice. ▶

I can ask and speculate about historical events. ✓

D Unexplained abilities

1 Reading 🎧

A "You don't remember what happened. What you remember becomes what happened." – John Green
What do you think this quote means? Do you trust your memory?

B Read the article. Do you think Jill Price views her ability as a gift or a curse?

THE WOMAN WHO CAN'T FORGET

Jill Price has a powerful memory. She can remember every detail of her life since age 14 — whether she wants to or not. "Since 1980, I remember everything." She remembers where she was, what she felt, what she was wearing, who she was with, what the weather was, and what was in the news.

When she contacted memory researchers in 2000, she was hopeful they could explain her abilities. But they were stumped. After lots of tests, the researchers identified a new medical condition for her called hyperthymesia, meaning "superior memory." Only a handful of people have been diagnosed with the condition.

Does she remember when the big plane crash in Scotland occurred? "December 21, 1988." Can she recall the first time she heard the song, "Jessie's Girl"? "March 7, 1981." She was driving in a car with her mother. Does she know what she was doing on August 29, 1980? "It was a Friday," she says. She went on a trip to the desert with her friends. Scientists have checked her memories against news reports and her own diaries. Her memories are right almost every time.

"I walk around with my life right next to me," said Price, who lives in California. "I always explain it to people like I'm walking around with a video camera on my shoulder. And every day is a videotape. So if you throw a date out at me, it's as if I pulled a videotape out...and just watch the day."

She doesn't remember everything — only things that happened in her own life. School was awful for her, she says, because she had problems remembering facts and numbers. "I can't look at a phone book and memorize names. I don't do that."

Sometimes she might like to forget, especially when bad things happen in her life. "I still feel bad about stuff that happened 30 years ago," Price said. "It's not as though I'm looking back on the events with the distance of time and adult perspective; it's as though I'm actually living through them again."

Price's condition reminds us that it's probable our happiness might not only depend on what we remember, but what we are able to forget.

C Read the story again. Answer the questions.

1 Since what year does Jill Price remember every day of her life? _____

2 What kinds of things does Jill remember? _____

3 What thing does Jill have trouble remembering? _____

4 How many people have been diagnosed with the same condition as Jill? _____

5 How does Jill describe the experience of remembering a day in her life? _____

6 How do scientists know her memory is correct? _____

D `PAIR WORK` Would you want to be able to remember everything? Why or why not?

2 **Listening** "The Magpies and the Bell"

A 🎧 Listen to a story from South Korea. Number the pictures from 1 to 6.

B 🎧 Listen again. Answer the questions.

1   Where was the man going?

2   Who was the woman that the man met at the house?

3   What did the snake tell the man to do?

4   Who saved the man? How? Why?

C What lesson about life do you think the story tells?

3 **Writing and speaking** A story

A Think of a story in your culture that explains something. What does it explain? How does the story explain it?

B Write the story, or retell the story in Exercise 2. Use the model paragraph to help you.

C GROUP WORK Share your stories. Are there any similarities among your stories? Are there any similarities to other stories you know?

The Sleep Tree, a Myth

One day, a man in the rain forest saw a huge, old tree he'd never seen before. Its roots went deep into the ground, and its branches spread all across the sky. The man was amazed. He saw a large group of animals sleeping under the old tree...

Wrap-up

1 Quick pair review

Lesson A | Do you remember?

How certain are the sentences? Write M (more certain) or L (less certain). You have one minute.

_____ 1 Tom might have been sick yesterday.

_____ 2 The glass must have fallen off the table and broken.

_____ 3 Wendy couldn't have had lunch with Michael yesterday.

_____ 4 Lola could have been at the party.

_____ 5 The storm might have started in Florida.

Lesson B | Give your opinion!

What do you think? Use phrases of probability and improbability.
Discuss your answers and give your reasons. You have two minutes.

1 Will cars run on water one day?

2 Will people be able to control the weather?

3 Will we find life on other planets?

A: Do you think cars will run on water one day?

B: It's highly unlikely. There isn't enough energy in water. What do you think?

Lesson C | Test your partner!

Say four questions. Can your partner write them as embedded questions?
Take turns. You have three minutes.

"Where is Sheila?"

1 _Do you know where Sheila is?_ ____   3 _____

2 _____   4 _____

Lesson D | Brainstorm!

Make up myths about one of the items with a partner. Be creative! You have three minutes.

why fish live in the ocean   why snakes don't have legs   why the sky is blue

A: A long time ago the sky was white, but a boy found blueberries, and threw
them in the sky. It turned the sky blue.

B: The sky was black, but when it rained for the first time, it turned blue.

2 In the real world

Why are these animals unusual? Go online and
find information in English about one of them.
Then write about them. What do they look like?
Where do they live? What do they eat?

- tree kangaroos
- magpies
- albino snakes
- wombats

Tree Kangaroos

Tree kangaroos are unusual because they
live in trees. They have shorter legs than
most kangaroos. They live in Australia and
Papua New Guinea.

10 Perspectives

Warm Up

A Look at the pictures. What do you see? What is the most unusual perspective?

B Do you always see things the same way as your friends?

A A traffic accident

1 Vocabulary Three-word phrasal verbs

A 🎧 **Match the statements in columns A and B. Then listen and check your answers.**

A

1 I like to **catch up with** friends online. _____
2 I can **come up with** imaginative ideas. _____
3 I **look up to** my father. _____
4 I **get along with** everybody. _____
5 It's hard to **keep up with** my friends. _____
6 I think that too many people **get away with** speeding. _____
7 I cannot **put up with** people who lie. _____
8 I try to **take care of** my car. _____
9 I always look forward to Sunday mornings. _____

B

a. I really respect him.
b. We chat several times a week.
c. I'm a very creative person.
d. The police should give more tickets.
e. People think I'm very friendly.
f. We don't have time to get together.
g. I change the oil every six months.
h. I love to sleep late on weekends.
i. I get very angry when people don't tell the truth.

B **PAIR WORK** **Which statements in Part A are true for you? Discuss your answers.**

"It's hard to keep up with my friends. I have a lot of friends because I get along with everybody."

2 Language in context Whose fault was it?

A 🎧 **Read the traffic accident report that the police officer wrote. What did the witness see?**

Traffic Accident Report

Mrs. Fran Perry, 35, hit a traffic light pole on the corner of First and Lexington at 6:45 this evening. She said she had turned quickly to avoid a dog. The pole was not damaged, but her car had a broken light. She said she would take care of it right away.

Mr. Jerry Thomas, 62, told an officer he'd seen the accident from his bedroom window. He saw a man who had taken his dog off its leash. He said the driver had been on her cell phone.

Both the driver and the witness said that they would come in and make a full statement.

B **What about you? Who do you feel is more responsible for the accident – the driver or the dog owner? Why?**

3 Grammar ∩ Reported statements

Use reported speech to tell what a speaker has said without using the person's exact words. When using reported speech, you often have to change pronouns and the tense of the verb.

Direct speech	Reported speech
"I **am** in a hurry."	She **told me** (that) she **was** in a hurry.
"I **am telling** the truth."	She **told me** (that) she **was telling** the truth.
"I **have** an appointment."	She **told me** (that) she **had** an appointment.
"I **saw** the accident."	He **said** (that) he **had seen** the accident.
"The dog **has disappeared**."	He **said** (that) the dog **had disappeared**.
"We **will make** a statement."	They **said** (that) they **would make** a statement.

A Complete the report with *said* or *told*. Then compare with a partner.

Car Accident on Main St.

Last night, Darren Jones, 18, was riding his bicycle when a car suddenly stopped in front of him. He crashed his bicycle into the car. Darren _____ police that he hadn't seen it stop. He _____ police he was sorry, but he _____ it hadn't been his fault. The driver, Lacey Reed, 45, _____ that she had stopped because a man was crossing the road. A witness, James Lee, 68, _____ police he had seen everything. Everyone _____ they would make a formal report.

B Rewrite these sentences. Use reported speech. Then compare with a partner.

1 Lacy said, "I want to call my husband."   *Lacey said she wanted to call her husband.*
2 Darren told me, "It's not my fault."   *Darren told me*
3 James told me, "I heard a loud crash." _____
4 James said, "I have seen accidents here before." _____
5 Lacey told me, "I'll take care of the bills." _____

4 Speaking What did he say?

A Choose one question. Write the answer in one sentence.

- What do you do to catch up with your friends?
- What are you looking forward to doing?
- How do you keep up with the news?

B GROUP WORK Whisper your sentence to the person on your right. That person whispers your sentence to the person on the right. Continue until the sentence is reported back to you. Was it your sentence, or was it different?

A: I'm looking forward to graduating next year.

B: Jason told me he was looking forward to graduating next year.

C: Maria said that Jason was looking forward to . . .

5 Keep talking!

Student A go to page 144 and
Student B go to page 146 for more practice.

I can report what people say. ☑   95

B As I was saying . . .

1 Interactions Changing and returning to the topic

A Do you enjoy sports? Which do you prefer, watching sports live or on TV? Why? Have you ever disagreed with a referee's call?

B 🎧 Listen to the conversation. What topics are they discussing? Then practice the conversation.

Maria   I don't believe it!

Kate   What?

Maria   He used his hands. That goal shouldn't have counted.

Kate   Are you sure he used his hands?

Maria   He did. I saw it clearly.

Kate   That reminds me, did you see the game last weekend? I didn't see it, but my brother told me that the same player had scored the winning goal. They won 1-0.

Maria   No, I missed it. But as I was saying, I don't think that was a real goal.

Kate   Maybe the referee just didn't see it. I know it happens sometimes.

Maria   That's possible. Referees are only human, after all.

C 🎧 Read the expressions below. Complete each box with a similar expression from the conversation. Then listen and check your answers.

Changing the topic	Returning to a topic
_____	_____
(By the way . . .)	(To finish what I was saying . . .)
(I just thought of something.)	(To get back to what I was saying . . .)

D Number the sentences from 1 to 6. Then practice with a partner.

_____ **A** I know. It was. I wish I could go to the game next Sunday, but I don't have tickets. And I have to –

_____ **A** I can't. Because to finish what I was saying, I have to study all weekend.

_____ **A** Did you see the soccer game last night?

_____ **B** I did. I watched it on TV. It was awesome.

_____ **B** That's too bad. But I have tickets for the game the following weekend, too. Want to go then?

_____ **B** Hang on. I just thought of something. I have two tickets! Want to go?

96

2 Pronunciation Linked vowel sounds with /w/ and /y/

A 🎧 Listen and repeat. Notice how the vowel sounds at the beginning and end of words are linked with a /w/ sound or a /y/ sound.

/w/	/w/	/w/	/y/	/y/	/y/
know if	do it	go over	say anything	see it	I am

B Listen. Write 'w' or 'y' over the linked sounds. Then practice with a partner.

/ /	/ /	/ /	/ /	/ /	/ /
pay any	how exactly	be in	too old	no one	who is

3 Listening Sports talk

A 🎧 Listen to three conversations between Alex and Celia. What do they discuss in each conversation? Check (✓) the answers.

What do they begin to discuss?	What is the topic changed to?
1 ☐ extreme sports ☐ the dangers of sports	
2 ☐ sports on TV ☐ the Olympics	
3 ☐ sports fads ☐ sports fans	

B 🎧 Listen again. What is the topic changed to in each conversation? Write the topics in the chart.

4 Speaking Stick to the topic

A 🎧 Choose one of these topics or another related to sports. Prepare to talk about it for at least a minute.

extreme sports	a great team
ads in sports	sports equipment
benefits of sports	sports fads
a great athlete	sports fans

B GROUP WORK Take turns. Discuss your topic. The other students keep trying to change the topic. Return to your topic each time.

A: I think snowboarding is an amazing extreme sport.

B: I agree. You know, that reminds me, did you see the ice skating at the Olympics this year?

A: Um, no. I couldn't watch the games. But as I was saying, snowboarding is really . . .

I can change and return to the topic. ✓

C There's always an explanation.

1 Vocabulary Verbs + prepositions

A 🎧 Match the verbs and the prepositions. Add the verbs to the chart. Then listen and check your answers.

believe	depend	forget	participate	rely
decide	dream	hear	plan	worry

about		on		in

B PAIR WORK Complete these questions with the correct prepositions. Ask and answer the questions. Do you see things the same way?

1 Do you believe _____ UFOs?

2 Who do you rely _____ the most?

3 What do you plan _____ doing in the future?

4 What's the most important news event you have heard _____ recently?

5 What did you dream _____ last night?

6 Do you participate _____ any community organizations?

2 Conversation Strange behavior

A 🎧 Listen to the conversation. Who do you think Chad is?

Gina   I'm worried. Chad's been acting strangely.

Marissa What do you mean?

Gina   Well, I asked him if he wanted to see a movie on Friday. He told me he couldn't, but he wouldn't say why.

Marissa That's odd.

Gina   Then last night he asked me if I was free for dinner on Saturday and if I'd ever been to Michel's.

Marissa I've heard about Michel's. It's one of the nicest places in town.

Gina   I know. We never go to places like that. We usually just get a pizza and sodas as takeout.

Marissa Well, I wouldn't worry about it. Just enjoy your dinner.

B 🎧 Listen to a phone conversation between Marissa and Chad. What did Chad do on Friday night? What's he planning to do on Saturday night?

3 Grammar ⌂ Reported *yes* / *no* questions

Use reported yes / no *questions to tell what a speaker has asked without using the person's exact words. When using reported* yes / no *questions you often have to change pronouns and the tense of the verb.*

Direct questions	Reported questions
"**Are** you free for dinner?"	He asked me if I **was** free for dinner.
"**Are** you **having** a good day?"	He asked me if I **was having** a good day.
"**Do** you **want** to see a movie?"	He asked me if I **wanted** to see a movie.
"**Did** you **speak** to your mother?"	He asked me if I **had spoken** to my mother.
"**Have** you **been** to Michel's?"	He asked me if I **had been** to Michel's.
"**Will** you **marry** me?"	He asked me if I **would marry** him.

Rewrite the questions. Use reported questions. Then compare with a partner.

1 Marissa asked Chad, "Have you spoken to Gina yet?"
   Marissa asked Chad if he had spoken to Gina yet.

2 Marissa asked Chad, "Are you planning on asking Gina to marry you?"
   _____

3 Marissa asked Chad, "Are you worried about Gina's answer?"
   _____

4 Chad asked Marissa, "Will Gina say yes?"
   _____

5 Gina asked Marissa, "Do you believe in love at first sight?"
   _____

6 Marissa asked Gina, "Did you dream about the perfect wedding as a child?"
   _____

7 Marissa asked Gina, "Have you already decided on a wedding date?"
   _____

4 Speaking Ask me anything!

A CLASS ACTIVITY **Imagine you are someone famous. Walk around the class. Find out who your classmates are. Ask and answer *yes* / *no* questions.**

A: Hello. I'm Will Smith.

B: Can I ask you a question? Do you participate in any charities?

B GROUP WORK **Report the most interesting questions and answers.**

"Francesca asked me if I participated in any charities. I told her I had participated in a lot of charities – especially ones that work with safe water."

5 Keep talking!

Go to page 145 for more practice.

I can report what people ask. ✓

D Seeing things differently

1 Reading 🎧

A What color is the dress below? How certain are you?

B Read the lecture by Professor Lin. What is the real color of the dress?

"THE DRESS" – A Lecture for Professor Lin's Psychology Class

Do you remember this meme from a few years ago? A young woman posted a picture of this dress online. She said she and her friends couldn't decide on what color it was. The image went viral. Within 10 hours, an online poll had received 1.8 million votes. About 72% of people reported that they saw white and gold and 28% saw black and blue. The question on everyone's mind was, how is that possible?

The dress is actually black and blue, but nearly three out of four people saw the wrong colors. *Here's why:*

Figure 1

Figure 2

Scientists think that our perception of color depends on our perception of lighting. For example, look at Figure 2 – the squares marked A and B are exactly the same color, but because the B square looks like it's in shadow and is where a lighter square should be, our brain tells us it's a lighter shade.

Now, looking at the picture of the dress, we don't know how it is lit. Is it natural light or artificial light? Is it in shadow? Our brains are really good at filling in details we don't know, so we make assumptions about the color of the lighting. People who assume the dress is in shadow or lit by natural light (which has more blue in it) tend to subtract the blue tones in the photo and see the dress as white and gold. People who assume the lighting is artificial (which has more yellow) assume the dress is black and blue.

The next question is, why do some people assume the dress is lit by natural light and others assume artificial light? Scientists think it may have to do with when we get up and go to sleep. People who are early risers spend more time in natural daylight and might assume the dress is lit by that same light. People who are night owls and are awake more at night might assume the dress is lit by the artificial light they spend more time in.

So the lesson is, whenever you're absolutely sure the way you see things is right, remember that there's a possibility that others have a perfectly good explanation for why they see it differently!

C Read the dialogue again. Answer the questions using reported speech.

1 Why did the original user post the photo?   *She said she and her friends couldn't decide on the color.*

2 How many votes did the poll receive?

3 How did scientists explain the difference in people's perception of color?

4 What did Professor Lin say our brains are really good at?

5 According to scientists, who might assume the dress is lit by artificial light?

D PAIR WORK What are other things that people see very differently? Can you imagine why they might have different opinions?

2 Listening Justin's turn

A 🎧 Listen to Allie ask her friend Justin some of the questions from a questionnaire. Number them from 1 to 5 in the order she asks them.

Questions	Answers
☐ What is your greatest fear?	
☐ What is your idea of perfect happiness?	
☐ What word do you most overuse?	
☐ What is your current state of mind?	
☐ What is your greatest regret?	

B 🎧 Listen again. Write Justin's answers.

3 Writing Questionnaire results

A Choose any two questions from Exercise 2, and write them in the chart. Think about your answers. Then ask each question to two classmates and write their answers.

	Questions	Name: _____	Name: _____
1			
2			

B Write about the questionnaire results in Part A. Use the model to help you.

> ### Questionnaire Results
>
> The three of us have very different regrets. Eun-ju said her greatest regret was quitting piano lessons. Antonio said that his was not listening to his grandfather's advice. I think my greatest regret is something I said to my brother once . . .

C GROUP WORK Share your writing with your classmates.

4 Speaking Imagine that!

A Look at the questions below. Think about your own answers.

- If you could have one superpower, what would it be?
- What famous person do you think you look like?
- What song title best describes your feelings about life?
- If you could be any animal for a day, what would you be?
- If a movie were made about your life, what would the title be?

B PAIR WORK Ask your partner the questions in Part A. Write the answers.

C GROUP WORK Report the most interesting information you found out.

I can discuss different perspectives. ✓

Wrap-up

1 Quick pair review

Lesson A Test your partner!

Say four sentences to your partner using direct speech. Can your partner say the sentences using reported speech? Take turns. You and your partner have one minute.

A: My sister will take *good care* of my *dog*.

B: You told me that your sister would take *good care* of your *dog*.

Lesson B Do you remember?

Complete the expressions for changing a topic and returning to a topic. Circle the correct words. You have one minute.

1 I **back** / **just** thought of something.

2 By the **way** / **what**, I saw a concert on Friday.

3 That **says** / **reminds** me, are you driving to work tomorrow?

4 As I was **saying** / **finishing** I look up to my teachers. They work very hard.

5 To finish **way** / **what** I was saying, let's have Chinese food.

6 To get **me** / **back** to what I was saying, Carly gets along with everybody.

Lesson C Find out!

Who is one person both you and your partner depend on? Worry about a lot? Have heard about recently in the news? Plan on visiting soon? You and your partner have two minutes.

A: I depend on my brother. He's older and knows a lot of things. What about you?

B: I don't have a brother. But I depend on my father. Do you?

A: Yes, I do.

Lesson D Give your opinion!

Who are people that you could describe using these phrases? You have two minutes.

a talented athlete _____	an amazing singer _____
a hardworking actor _____	a quick thinker _____
a friendly teacher _____	a confident woman _____

2 In the real world

Whose side are you on? Go online and find information in English about one of these topics. Then write about it. What do people think about it? What do you think?

- art made from recycled trash
- extreme sports
- hybrid cars
- reality shows

Trash Art

Many people think art made from recycled trash is good for the environment. Other people think it's ugly.

I agree with both opinions. It is good for the environment, but it's usually ugly!

11 The real world

Warm Up

A Match the jobs and the pictures.

1 animal trainer
2 archaeologist
3 DJ
4 fashion designer
5 hairstylist
6 race-car driver
7 singer / songwriter
8 tour guide
9 social media marketer

B What three jobs do you think would be the most interesting? What would you like about them? Why?

Getting it done

1 **Vocabulary** Word partners

A 🎧 Cross out the words that do not go together. Then listen and check your answers.

1	accept	a job offer / ~~a job ad~~
2	apply for	a letter / a job
3	format	an interview / a résumé
4	prepare for	a business card / an interview
5	print	an email / a job
6	proofread	a résumé / a job offer
7	provide	a company / references
8	research	a job / a résumé
9	send	a thank-you note / a phone call
10	translate	a job / a letter

B PAIR WORK Ask and answer the questions.

1 If you were looking for a job, what things in Part A would you do?

2 Have you ever applied for a job? What was it?

3 What would you include on your résumé?

2 **Language in context** Tips from a recruiter

A 🎧 Read the tips from a recruiter to job hunters. Which tip should you do after the interview?

Find references
Get people that you trust to provide references for you.

Invest in your résumé
Get your résumé formatted, proofread, and printed on good quality paper.

Prepare for the interview
Have a friend prepare possible interview questions. Practice answering them

Know the way
Research directions to the interview site and have someone drive you there.

Don't be late
Arrive at the interview site at least 15 minutes before the interview.

Look your best
Have your best clothes dry-cleaned and pressed. Dress for success!

Remember to smile
Show a pleasant face the minute you walk into the interview. Keep smiling.

Do the research
Research the job and the company. Ask questions about information that is not found on the company's website.

Say thanks
Send a short thank-you note or email to the person or people who interviewed you.

B What about you? Are all the tips appropriate in your culture? What other tips can you add?

3 Grammar ∩ Causative *get* and *have*

get + someone + to + *verb*	get + something + *past participle*
Get people to **provide** references for you.	Where can I **get** my résumé **printed**?
get + someone + *verb*	Have + something + *past participle*
I plan to **have** a friend **practice** with me.	I need to **have** my clothes **dry-cleaned**.

A Circle the correct words. Then compare with a partner.

1 My company is trying to get Greg **accept** / **to accept** / **accepted** our job offer.

2 I need to have someone **translate** / **to translate** / **translated** my résumé into English.

3 I'd like to get my former boss **provide** / **to provide** / **provided** a reference letter.

4 You should have your suit **dry-clean** / **to dry-clean** / **dry-cleaned** before the interview.

5 Where can I get some business cards **print** / **to print** / **printed**?

B Put the words in order. Then compare with a partner.

1 Paul / his brother / gets / his hair / cut / to   Paul _gets his brother to cut his hair_ .

2 I / to / a reference letter / got / write / my boss   I _____ .

3 Where / have / proofread / I / can / my résumé   Where _____ ?

4 Jay / his house / on Saturday / had / cleaned   Jay _____ .

5 Liz / to get / proofread / her presentation / needs   Liz _____ .

4 Listening So much to do!

A ∩ Listen to three busy people talk about their plans. Write what they are going to do themselves.

	Do themselves	Have or get done
1		
2		
3		

B ∩ Listen again. Write one thing each person is going to have or get done.

5 Speaking Do it yourself?

GROUP WORK Imagine you are preparing for an interview. Look at the "to do" list. What would you do yourself? What would you have or get done? Share your ideas.

○ cut my hair	iron my shirt	proofread my résumé
○ dry-clean my suit	photocopy my résumé	take photos
○ format my résumé	print business cards	translate my résumé

A: I'd format my résumé, but I'd get someone else to proofread it.

B: Me, too. I'd have my résumé translated, and then I'd photocopy it myself.

6 Keep talking!

Go to page 147 for more practice.

I can talk about getting things done. ✓   105

B Let me see . . .

1 Interactions Interviewing

A Imagine you've applied for a job at a company and are preparing for an interview. What topics do you think you would discuss in the interview?

benefits	hours	salary	your education
break times	retirement plan	travel opportunities	your skills and abilities

B 🎧 Listen to the conversation. How does Mr. Reed describe himself? Practice the conversation.

Interviewer	I just have a few more questions, Mr. Reed. Why do you want to work here?
Mr. Reed	I'd like to get some experience in this field and put my skills to work.
Interviewer	And what are your best skills?
Mr. Reed	Oh, let's see. . .I'm responsible, hardworking, and can work independently.
Interviewer	That's good. Can you work weekends?
Mr. Reed	Sure. That's not a problem.
Interviewer	Can you provide references?
Mr. Reed	Of course.
Interviewer	Well, it's been nice meeting you. I want to thank you for coming in for this interview.
Mr. Reed	Thank you very much.

C 🎧 Read the expressions below. Complete each box with a similar expression from the conversation. Then listen and check your answers.

Taking time to think	Closing an interview
_____	_____
Um, let me see . . .	Well, it's been great talking to you.
Hmm, let me think . . .	Well, I've really enjoyed talking to you.

D Number the sentences from 1 to 8. Then practice with a partner.

_____	A	You're welcome. We'll be in touch.	B	Thank you for the interview.
__1__	A	So, what skills do you have?	B	Good-bye. Thank you again.
_____	A	Good. Well, it's been nice meeting you.	B	Um, let me see. I could start in a week.
_____	A	That's good. What's the earliest you can start?	B	I'm good with people, and I can use all of the latest office software.

2 Listening Getting the job?

A 🎧 Listen to the last part of a job interview. Check (✓) the job the man is most likely applying for.

☐ TV host ☐ soccer coach ☐ radio DJ ☐ translator ☐ scientist

B Listen again. How does the man answer the interviewer's questions? Complete the interviewer's notes.

1 What skills do you have? _____ and asking questions
2 What would you like about the job? the _____ _____
3 What is your greatest strength? _____ skills
4 What is your greatest weakness? doesn't _____ some current _____
5 What is your career goal? host TV _____ _____
6 Can you work weekends? can work _____ but not _____

C PAIR WORK Did the man interview well? Why or why not?

3 Speaking Help wanted

A Prepare for a job interview. Choose one of the jobs. Think of answers to the questions below.

JOBS

MAGAZINE COLUMNIST

Trendy magazine seeks outgoing person to write weekly column on what's hot around town. Latest knowledge of music, food, movies, and fashion required. Must be able to write quickly under pressure. Pay per word.

ASSISTANT COACH

Energetic and patient person needed to work as part-time assistant to head coach at local high school. No experience necessary. Strong ability in several sports desired. Applicant must be a team player. Pay negotiable.

ONLINE TUTOR

Work from home! Reliable tutor needed to teach English and / or math to high school students online. Must have own phone and computer and be able to work independently. Flexible hours. Hourly pay. Perfect for college students.

- Can you tell me a little about yourself?
- What skills do you have?
- What is your greatest strength?
- What is your greatest weakness?
- What is your career goal?
- Can you work weekends?
- How would your friends describe you?
- How do you cope with stress?

B PAIR WORK Role-play the job interview for a job in Part A. Then change roles.

Student A: Tell your partner which job you have chosen. Answer Student B's questions. Take time to think when you need to.

Student B: Interview Student A. Ask the questions in Part A and questions of your own. Then close the interview.

I can take time to think in an interview. ✓
I can close an interview. ✓

C Future goals

1 Vocabulary Setting goals

A 🎧 Match the words and the pictures. Then listen and check your answers.

a	be financially independent	c	have a big wedding	e	prepare for my exams	g	work as a journalist
b	do volunteer work	d	live in the countryside	f	study abroad	h	write travel books

 1 ☐
 2 ☐
 3 ☐
 4 ☐

 5 ☐
 6 ☐
 7 ☐
 8 ☐

B **PAIR WORK** Do you have any of these goals? Which ones? Have you already reached any of these goals? Tell your partner.

2 Conversation Planning ahead

A 🎧 Listen to the conversation. Who will Zac marry in five years?

Zac Guess what! I've decided to study abroad next year. At this time next year, I'll be studying in Paris!

Lucy Really? That sounds wonderful.

Zac I've been thinking a lot lately about what I want to achieve in my life. In five years, I'll be working as a journalist. In seven years, I'll be living in the countryside. In twenty years –

Lucy But what about family? Will you get married?

Zac Oh, yes. I'll have a big wedding in five years.

Lucy OK . . . and who will you marry?

Zac I have no idea. But I'm sure I'll meet someone.

B 🎧 Listen to the rest of the conversation. What two things is Lucy doing these days? What job does she think she'll have in five years?

3 Grammar 🎧 Future continuous vs. future with *will*

> *Use the future continuous form to describe actions in progress at a specific time in the future.*
> Where **will** you **be studying** next year?
>   **I'll be studying** in Paris. I **won't be working** as a journalist then.
>
> *Use the future with* will *verbs that are not usually used in the continuous form.*
> What **will** you **achieve** in twenty years? **Will** you **be** financially independent?
>   Yes, I **will**. But I**'ll have to** work really hard.

**Complete the conversations with the future continuous or future with *will*.
Then practice with a partner.**

1 A What _____ you _____ (do) a year from now?

   B I _____ (study) abroad.

2 A What _____ (happen) to your friends after graduation?

   B Sam and Ann _____ (have) a big wedding. Jacob

      _____ (work) in the city.

3 A Where _____ you _____ (live) in ten years?

   B I don't know, but I probably _____ (not / live) here.

4 A What _____ your life _____ (be) like in the future?

   B I _____ (not / work) for a large company. I

      _____ (write) travel books.

5 A _____ you _____ (go) on vacation in July?

   B Yes, I _____ (go) to Rome. I _____ (see)

      the Colosseum and the Trevi Fountain.

4 Pronunciation Reduction of *will*

A 🎧 **Listen and repeat. Notice how *will* often gets reduced to 'll after
Wh- question words and nouns.**

When will your friends finish this class? What will they be doing afterwards?

John will still be studying, and Beth will be looking for a job.

B PAIR WORK **Practice the questions and answers in Exercise 3A. Pay attention
to the reduction of *will*.**

5 Speaking My own goals

A What goals do you have? When do you hope to reach those goals?

B GROUP WORK **Share your goals. Ask and answer questions to get
more information.**

A: I'll be married in five years. I think I'll be working for a large company.

B: What kind of large company will you be working for?

6 Keep talking!

Go to page 148 for more practice.

I can ask and talk about future goals. ✓

D My career

1 Reading 🎧

A The jobs of today may not be the jobs of the future. Which of these jobs do you think will exist in the future? Will they be different in any way? Which will disappear? Why?

| cashier | doctor | farmer | pilot | reporter | soldier | teacher | travel agent |

B Read the article. What is it about? Check (✓) the main idea.

☐ jobs that will appear ☐ jobs that will disappear ☐ current jobs that will stay the same

JOBS OF THE FUTURE

Drone Manager – More businesses and government agencies will be relying on drones to take video from the air, or even to deliver packages. Companies will need drone managers to keep track of all their drones, to make sure they operate within the law and don't cause damage or injuries.

Rewilder – Rewilders will help to repair environmental damage by returning developed areas to their natural state. From tearing down buildings and ripping up roads to replacing industrial areas with forests, rewilders will be undoing the damage that buildings, cars, factories, and human beings have done to the planet.

Robot Technician – Nearly half of all jobs today will be taken over by robots during this century. Companies will have robots to repair watches, make phone calls, sew clothing, and handle many other routine tasks. Robot programmers and technicians will be needed to tell the robots what to do and to take care of the mechanical problems that these robots will certainly have.

Space Tour Guide – More and more people will be taking vacations in space, and they will need tour guides. Several companies have already begun space programs with trips that cost between $75,000 and $2 million. In the future, these high prices should become more affordable, and more space guides will be needed.

Organ Designers – Millions of people today are waiting for new hearts, lungs, livers, and other organs. In the future, organ manufacturers will be making artificial organs, organs grown in a laboratory from a patient's own cells, or combinations of both. Organs will be designed to fit each individual patient.

C Check (✓) the true sentences. Then correct the false ones.

☐ 1 A drone manager may be a needed job in the future. _____

☐ 2 Rewilders will help build new roads and factories. _____

☐ 3 Robots will take over almost all future jobs. _____

☐ 4 Space travel for tourists has already begun. _____

☐ 5 Organs will be made only from a patient's own cells. _____

D **PAIR WORK** Which of the jobs in the article do you think is most likely to be a popular career? What qualifications would someone need for these jobs? Discuss your ideas.

2 **Writing and speaking** A letter of interest

A Read these job ads for positions at Carolina Industries. Then read the letter below. What job is Teresa interested in?

Tech Support Officer
Maintain and ensure smooth running of computer systems and internal network. Must be familiar with latest hardware and software. Flexible hours.

Recruiter
Find, interview, and test applicants to locate qualified employees for job openings. Must be organized and able to travel to colleges and job fairs.

Marketing Assistant
Entry-level job for recent graduate. Assist staff in Marketing Department. Duties include filing, research, and working with new customers.

Your address	Portal Bravo #19D 37529 Leon, Mexico
Date	June 7, 2019
Name, title, company, and address of the person you're writing to	Ms. Susan Dodd Personnel Manager Carolina Industries 662 Beacon Road Salt Lake City, Utah 84110
Try to use the name of the person.	Dear Ms. Dodd:
State why you are writing.	I would like to express my interest in the marketing assistant job recently advertised on your website.
Briefly state your education and any experience or skills.	I will be graduating next month with a B.A. in Marketing from Monterrey University. I am fluent in English and Spanish, with a basic knowledge of Japanese. Enclosed is my résumé, which contains detailed information on my education and experience.
Say how you can be contacted.	I would appreciate the opportunity to discuss this position with you. I can be reached by cell phone at 319-555-8116 or by email at teresasanchez@cup.org.
Thank the person.	Thank you very much for your time and consideration.
Use a formal closing.	Sincerely,
Sign your name.	Theresa Sanchez Theresa Sanchez

B Choose a job from this lesson or use your own idea. Write a letter of interest.

C GROUP WORK Share your letters. What kinds of jobs are your classmates interested in? What do you think they will be doing in five years?

A: Jean is interested in the tech support job.

B: Really? I think Jean will be working as a space tour guide in the future, not a tech support officer. She's so friendly and outgoing.

I can discuss future careers.

Wrap-up

1 Quick pair review

Lesson A Find out!

What are two things both you and your partner usually have done or get done?
You and your partner have two minutes.

A: I get my photos printed at the drugstore.

B: Really? I print my pictures on my computer. I usually have my nice clothes dry-cleaned. What about you?

A: Yes. I do, too.

Lesson B Do you remember?

What can you say when you need time to think? Check (✓) the correct answers.
You have one minute.

_____ 1 Oh, let's see.

_____ 2 Well, it's been great talking to you.

_____ 3 I'm not sure that's really true.

_____ 4 Oh, really?

_____ 5 Um, let me see.

_____ 6 Hmm, let me think.

Lesson C Guess!

Describe something you will be doing in the future, but don't say where it will be.
Can your partner guess the place? You have two minutes.

A: I'll be sitting in the sun in two months, and I'll be swimming in the ocean.

B: Will you be on vacation? Will you be going to the beach?

A: Yes, I will.

Lesson D Give your opinion!

How important will these jobs be in 50 years? Rank them from 1 (the most important)
to 8 (the least important). Compare your answers. You have three minutes.

_____ computer programmer	_____ lawyer
_____ librarian	_____ TV host
_____ English teacher	_____ flight attendant
_____ art teacher	_____ chef

2 In the real world

How can you prepare for jobs of the future? Go to a university website.
See what classes they offer, such as video-game design, robotics, or solar
energy. Then write about a job of the future.

Preparing for Jobs of the Future

In the future, most jobs will be high-tech. Everyone will have to study math and science to get a good job. I want to design video games, so I will . . .

12 Finding solutions

"It's just their little way of saying, 'Sorry we wrecked the planet.'"

Warm Up

A Describe the cartoons. What are the problems in each cartoon?

B How do you feel about the problems?

A Environmental concerns

1 Vocabulary Preventing pollution

A 🎧 Match the **bold** words and their meanings. Then listen and check your answers.

Ways of preventing air pollution

1 **Combine** tasks if you drive. _____
2 **Commute** by bicycle if possible. _____
3 **Maintain** your car so that it's more efficient. _____
4 **Avoid** products that come in spray cans. _____

a. don't use
b. go to work
c. do together
d. keep in good condition

Ways of preventing water pollution

5 **Store** paint and chemicals in safe containers. _____
6 **Limit** your use of harmful cleaning products. _____
7 **Discard** paint and batteries properly. _____
8 **Conserve** water whenever possible. _____

e. save
f. put or keep
g. throw away
h. control the amount

Ways of preventing land pollution

9 **Purchase** products with little packaging. _____
10 **Recycle** any item you can. _____
11 **Identify** where trash cans are. _____
12 Never **dump** motor oil on the ground. _____

i. use again
j. find or locate
k. put carelessly
l. buy

B **PAIR WORK** Which things in Part A do you think you could do? Which do you already do? Tell your partner.

2 Language in context Promoting "green" travel

A 🎧 Read about a high-tech solution to traveling "green." What problem did it solve?

Bicycles are being parked in a whole new way in Tokyo. Commuters used to leave their bicycles on the sidewalks outside train stations, but people couldn't move around them and something clearly had to be done. Now, at Kasai Station, commuters can leave their bikes in a 10-level underground parking garage that is controlled by robots. Robots store nearly 10,000 bicycles a day. When commuters want their bicycles, they use cards to identify them. Within seconds, a robot finds and brings it to them. The Tokyo garage is so successful that more "green" garages are being considered.

B How does the underground parking garage help "green" travel? Could Tokyo's solution work for you?

3 Grammar ∩ Present continuous passive; infinitive passive

> Use the present continuous passive to describe an action in progress when you want
> to focus on the receiver of the action instead of on the doer of the action.
>
> *Active*
> Commuters **are parking** bicycles in a new way.
>
> *Passive*
> Bicycles **are being parked** in a new way.
>
> Use the infinitive passive after verbs like have and need when you want to focus on
> the receiver of the action instead of the doer of the action.
>
> *Active*
> Somebody **had to do** something.
> People **needed to put** the bikes somewhere.
>
> *Passive*
> Something **had to be done**.
> The bikes **needed to be put** somewhere.

A Rewrite these sentences in the passive. Then compare with a partner.

1 People are reusing more items every day. _____

2 People need to maintain cars for safety. _____

3 Guests are conserving water in hotels. _____

4 You have to discard old batteries properly. _____

5 Homeowners need to store chemicals safely. _____

B Complete the sentences with the present continuous passive or the infinitive passive.
Then compare with a partner.

The Billabong clothing company has found an unusual way to
make clothes. Plastic soda bottles and discarded clothing
_____ (combine) to make "eco-friendly" shorts.
The company says that with this new material, environmental
pollution _____ (limit). For example, ten recycled
bottles have _____ (use) to make one pair of
Billabong shorts; that means ten fewer bottles in landfills. Currently,
the shorts _____ (sell) for about $50.

4 Speaking Environmental trends

A Which trends are happening in your town, city, or country? Check (✓) your answers.

☐ More products are being reused.

☐ More water is being conserved.

☐ The air is becoming less polluted.

☐ More hybrid cars are being purchased.

☐ Money is being spent on "green" technology.

☐ More solar energy is being produced.

B GROUP WORK Compare your answers. What do you think is causing each trend?
Choose one trend that is not happening. What do you think needs to be done about it?

5 Keep talking!

Go to page 149 for more practice.

I can discuss environmental trends.

B That's a good point.

1 Interactions Opinions

A Do you do any of these activities when you travel? How could these activities affect the environment?

bicycling	camping	hiking	kayaking	snorkeling	viewing wildlife

B 🎧 Listen to the conversation. Where does Daniela want to stay on vacation? Then practice the conversation.

Elena Where are you going on vacation?

Daniela Maybe to this eco-friendly resort.

Elena What do you mean, "eco-friendly"?

Daniela Well, it combines eco-tourism and helping the local community. It's important to be responsible when you travel, don't you think?

Elena That's a good point.

Daniela So, this place looks good. They're trying to conserve water. And they want you to purchase handmade objects from the local businesses.

Elena Do you know who owns it?

Daniela I have no idea. Why do you ask?

Elena Well, some eco-resorts are owned by big companies, so the money they make doesn't help the local community very much.

Daniela I don't see it that way. Eco-resorts give jobs to local people and help raise environmental awareness, no matter who owns them.

C 🎧 Read the expressions below. Complete each box with a similar expression from the conversation. Then listen and check your answers.

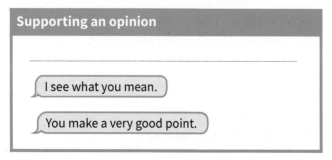

Supporting an opinion

_____

I see what you mean.

You make a very good point.

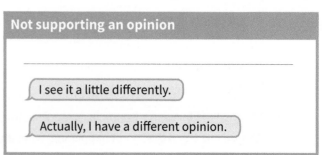

Not supporting an opinion

_____

I see it a little differently.

Actually, I have a different opinion.

D PAIR WORK Share your opinions about eco-tourism Use the ideas below or your own idea. Support or don't support one another's opinions.

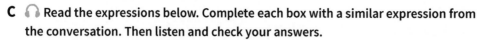

builds environmental awareness	helps locals more than it hurts them
can actually damage the environment	is only a trendy marketing word

2 Listening A case for tap water?

A 🎧 Listen to the conversation between Eric and Mandy about bottled water. Number the pictures from 1 to 4.

B 🎧 Listen again. Complete the sentences with the correct numbers.

1 People in the U.S. spend more than _____ billion dollars a year on bottled water.

2 More than _____ % of bottled water is just tap water.

3 People are drinking _____ % more bottled water every year.

4 Manufacturing bottles uses _____ times the amount of water in the bottle.

5 The energy used to make plastic bottles can drive _____ million cars a year.

6 People in the U.S. buy _____ billion bottles of water a year.

7 Only _____ % of the bottles are being recycled.

8 It only costs _____ cents a gallon to get tap water in your home.

C **PAIR WORK** Does Eric approve of buying bottled water? How do you feel about buying bottled water?

3 Speaking Seeing both sides

GROUP WORK Check (✓) the opinions you agree with. Then compare and discuss your opinions.

☐ Schools should be required to serve only healthy food.

☐ Kids at school should be free to eat whatever food they want.

☐ Rich countries have to pay more to fight climate change.

☐ Every country has to pay more to fight climate change.

☐ The worst kind of pollution is air pollution.

☐ The worst kind of pollution is water pollution.

☐ The worst kind of pollution is land pollution.

A: I think the worst kind of pollution is air pollution. If the air is dirty, people can't breathe.

B: I see it a little differently. Water pollution is worse because . . .

I can take time to think in an interview. ✓

C My community

1 Vocabulary Community improvement

A 🎧 **Complete the sentences. Then listen and check your answers.**

1 A **beautiful project** makes a community _____ .
   a. more attractive   b. less attractive

2 At a **community garden**, people _____ .
   a. can go camping   b. grow vegetables or flowers

3 At an **employment center**, people can get _____ .
   a. job information   b. marriage advice

4 At a **health clinic**, people can get medical _____ .
   a. problems   b. help

5 With a **neighborhood watch**, neighbors try to limit _____ .
   a. crime   b. pollution

6 A **public library** is used by _____ .
   a. members only   b. everyone

7 A **recreation center** is a place to _____ .
   a. help build homes   b. play sports or games

8 A **recycling center** is a place to _____ .
   a. take used materials   b. get housing advice

B PAIR WORK **Which services in Part A do you have in your community? What other services do you have in your community? Who do these services help?**

A: I know we have a public library, a health clinic, and a recreation center.

B: But I don't think there's a community garden.

2 Conversation A better place to live

A 🎧 **Listen to the conversation. Who will a recreation center help?**

Interviewer	Hi. I'm with the community improvement board.
Mr. Brown	Great. You guys are doing a fantastic job.
Interviewer	Thank you. As you know, we no longer have a community garden because of a lack of interest. Would you want to build a recreation center instead?
Mr. Brown	That's a good idea. We should build one so teens have a place to go.
Interviewer	OK. Now, although we have a neighborhood watch, there's still crime. So we're planning on putting video cameras on streetlights –
Mr. Brown	Great. There goes our privacy.
Interviewer	So you won't support these cameras?

B 🎧 **Listen to the rest of the conversation. Which community improvement would Mr. Brown support? Which one wouldn't he support?**

3 Grammar 🎧 Linking words

Reason:	We no longer have a community garden **because of** a lack of interest.
Result:	There's still crime, **so** we're planning to install video cameras.
Contrast:	**Although** we have a neighborhood watch, there's still crime.
Condition:	Teens will have a place to go **if** we build a recreation center.
Purpose:	We should build a recreation center **so (that)** teens have a place to go.

A Circle the correct words. Then compare with a partner.

1 The city stopped all beautification projects **because of** / **so that** a lack of money.

2 Why don't you visit the employment center **if** / **so that** you need a job?

3 Let's go to the public library **because of** / **so that** we can borrow some books.

4 I'm not feeling well, **although** / **so** I'm going to go to the health clinic.

5 **Although** / **So** we have a community garden, few people know about it.

6 Crime in our community is down **because of** / **so that** the neighborhood watch.

B PAIR WORK Complete these sentences with your own ideas.

Although our town is safe, . . .	If you want a place to relax, . . .
I have a bag of empty cans, so . . .	We need to make changes because of . . .

4 Pronunciation Rise-falling and low falling tones

🎧 **Listen and repeat. Notice the rise-falling and low falling tones in the responses. A rise-falling tone means you really mean what you're saying. A low falling tone can mean that you don't mean what you're saying.**

A I'm with the community board.　　　B Great. You guys are doing a fantastic job.

A We're putting in video cameras.　　　B Great. There goes our privacy.

5 Speaking Quality of life

GROUP WORK How can you improve the quality of life for these people in your community? Share your ideas.

children	families	teenagers
the elderly	new arrivals	unemployed people

"Although there's playground equipment in the park, it's old. So I think we should raise money for new equipment."

6 Keep talking!

Go to page 150 for more practice.

I can discuss ways to improve my community. 119

D Getting involved

1 Reading 🎧

A What are some of the challenges young people face today?

B Read the article. According to Dr. Abreu, how can orchestra training help with the problems that children in poor neighborhoods face?

04/10/18

El Sistema: Social Change Through Music

In 1975, Dr. José Abreu, a musician and economist, wanted to do something about the poverty, violence, and hopelessness that many children experienced in his home nation of Venezuela. So he started an orchestra training program for children, known today as El Sistema.

It was not an obvious solution. At the time, there were just two orchestras in the entire country, and a classical music audience of only about 1,000. But Abreu believed that daily music instruction after school in a safe place would help protect children from violence on the streets. He thought that playing and learning together as a group could give children a sense of community and help them to learn to live in harmony with others. As Abreu says, "The orchestra is the only group that comes together with the sole purpose of agreement."

El Sistema is very different than most music programs. In traditional music education, a student might have one lesson each week for 30 minutes. In El Sistema, students study three to four hours every day. El Sistema students play and study in groups, rather than practicing alone.

Every learner is expected to be a teacher—once students have mastered a skill, it is their responsibility and privilege to teach it to another student. And while many music programs are available only to the best musicians, El Sistema is free and open to any child who wants to participate and work hard to improve.

The impact of this program is remarkable. Venezuela today has hundreds of orchestras for children, youth, and adults, and hundreds of thousands of children are being given daily music education. El Sistema has spread to 60 countries throughout the world. Although most who participate in El Sistema will not become professional musicians, the program is helping countless children gain a sense of accomplishment, develop strong social connections, and build creative and leadership skills.

C Read the article again. Answer the questions.

1 Why did Dr. Abreu start El Sistema? _____

2 What does playing music together help children to do? _____

3 How much time do students study each day? _____

4 Who may join an El Sistema program? _____

5 What skills is El Sistema helping to build? _____

D PAIR WORK How might this program change the adults and children who participate in it? Discuss your ideas.

2 **Writing** A letter to a community leader

A Write a letter to a community leader about an issue that you feel needs to be addressed. Use these questions and the model to help you.

- Who are you?
- What is the issue?
- What is currently being done?
- What needs to be done?

B PAIR WORK Exchange letters with a partner. Do you agree?

> ### Dear Councilman Perez,
>
> I am a third-year student at Union University. I am writing to express my concern about how difficult it is for people in wheelchairs to enter many buildings on campus. Although some public buildings have wheelchair ramps, most do not. The city needs to require that all buildings have ramps. . . .

3 **Listening** Helping out

A 🎧 Listen to three people talk about issues. Check (✓) the issue they're involved in.

	Issue	What they're doing to help
Fernando *Fortaleza, Brazil*	☐ translating ☐ job training	
Aicha *Casablanca, Morocco*	☐ beautification projects ☐ parking issues	
Ingrid *Düsseldorf, Germany*	☐ helping new arrivals ☐ recreation centers	

B 🎧 Listen again. What are they doing to help? Write one example in the chart.

C Which issue in Part A are you concerned about? What other ways can people help?

4 **Speaking** Raising awareness

A Work with a partner. Agree on a charity, a cause, or an organization you would like people to be aware of. Then plan a way to raise awareness of the problem or its solution. Consider these ideas and ideas of your own.

> organize a community event
>
> create a social networking group
>
> give presentations at schools
>
> have a contest to raise money
>
> pass out information on the street
>
> put up informational posters around town
>
> run public-service announcements on the radio
>
> set up an information table on the sidewalk
>
> set up an email marketing campaign

B CLASS ACTIVITY Share your ideas with the class. Ask and answer questions for more information.

I can discuss ways to raise awareness. ✓

Wrap-up

1 Quick pair review

Lesson A   Do you remember?

Match the active and passive sentences. You have one minute.

1 You need to limit your use of running water. _____

2 Our building is limiting our use of running water. _____

3 The office store is discarding printer ink. _____

4 You need to discard your printer ink at an office store. _____

5 You have to purchase "green" items online. _____

a. Your printer ink needs to be discarded at an office store.

b. Our use of running water is being limited.

c. "Green" items have to be purchased online.

d. Printer ink is being discarded by the office store.

e. Your use of running water needs to be limited.

Lesson B   Give your opinion!

What do you think about these eco-friendly activities? Use expressions to support or not support your partner's opinion. You and your partner have two minutes.

Avoid using plastic bags.	Don't purchase a new cell phone every year.
Buy energy saving lightbulbs.	Take your own bags to a store.
Don't dump paint.	Walk to work.

A: Don't dump paint.

B: That's a good point. Recycle it. For example, give it to a friend to use.

Lesson C   Brainstorm!

Make a list of community improvement ideas. How many can you remember? You have two minutes.

Lesson D   Find out!

Who are two people that both you and your partner think are role models? You and your partner have two minutes.

2 In the real world

What is a problem in your community? Go online and find information about one of these problems, or choose your own idea. Find out about possible solutions. Then write about it.

- parking
- pollution
- traffic
- trash

Trash

People dump trash everywhere. There aren't enough trash cans for people to throw things away in. Trash cans need to be put on every corner in every city.

You've got to have this!

A Read the ads below. Choose one. Make a list of reasons to buy the product. Use these ideas and your own ideas.

Flying alarm clock
Can't get up in the morning? When this alarm clock goes off, it flies around the room. You have to get out of bed to turn it off.

Keyboard waffle maker
Say good-bye to boring old waffles. This waffle maker makes the tasty breakfast treat in the shape of computer keyboards.

Bakery flash drives
Flash drives are such a great way to carry data. But why not make yours a little more interesting with these bakery items?

Gel ant house
Ants can be a little boring to watch – but not when they live in this world of green gel. When the ants move, the gel changes colors.

Mini motorcycle
Motorcycles have one wheel in front of the other, but this one has two side by side. Just turn it on, lean forward and go!

Umbrella light
No more walking home in the dark. This umbrella has a light inside. Just turn it on and you have a light – and a safe walk home.

B PAIR WORK Take turns. Describe your product from Part A. Try to convince your partner to buy the product.

"The umbrella light is such a convenient product that all of your friends will want one. You can keep it in your bag. It's so useful that you will never leave home without it."

C PAIR WORK Would you buy your partner's product? Would you buy any of the products? Why or why not? Share your ideas.

Product improvements

A `PAIR WORK` Choose a product. What is it used for? What features does it have? Brainstorm all the things the product does.

car	coffeemaker	hair dryer	refrigerator
cell phone	computer	headphones	TV

A: A cell phone is used to call people.

B: They're used to check the time, text people, and . . .

B `PAIR WORK` Re-design your product. What words describe your product? What improvements have you made to your product? How is it used now?

C `GROUP WORK` Present your product to another pair.

A: We have developed a creative and useful product.

B: It is a flying car. It is terrific in traffic, and it will be very successful someday.

Keep talking!

Lucky Larry

A `PAIR WORK` **Make a story. Number the pictures from 1 to 9.**

☐ Some people were moving a piano into the upstairs apartment, but they hadn't gotten it inside yet.

☐ It took a long time to get home. Earlier, a police officer had stopped him for speeding.

☐ He was very thankful that he hadn't been in the car at the time.

☐ He went to the concert with Gail because she'd given him the tickets for his birthday.

☐ He then realized he hadn't taken his umbrella from his apartment.

☐ By the time he parked his car in front of his apartment, it had started to rain.

☐ After he'd locked his car, he ran to the front door in the rain.

1 Larry drove home one evening. He'd been at a piano concert with his friend Gail.

☐ He heard a very loud noise, so he turned around. The piano had fallen on his car!

B `GROUP WORK` **Join another pair. Take turns. Tell your stories. Are they the same?**

C `GROUP WORK` **Close your books. Tell the story in your own words from memory.**

A different path?

A Read the topics in each box. Check (✓) three that were important moments in your life. Write an example of each and why these moments were important.

"If I hadn't gone to summer camp, I wouldn't have met my best friend."

"I bought a new computer last summer, and now I can work from home."

Important moments in life	Examples and explanations
☐ a job you got ☐ a job you didn't get	
☐ someone you met who changed your life ☐ someone you wish you hadn't met	
☐ something you said to a friend ☐ something you didn't say to a friend	
☐ a place you visited ☐ a place you didn't visit	
☐ something you bought ☐ something you didn't buy	
☐ an exam you passed ☐ an exam you didn't pass	
☐ something you learned to do ☐ something you didn't learn to do	
☐ other: (your own idea)	

B **GROUP WORK** Take turns. Talk about the important moments in your chart. Ask each other questions for more details. Then find out: How would things have been different without these moments?

A: One time, I missed my plane to Los Angeles.

B: Why were you going to Los Angeles?

A: I had an interview for an internship.

C: Why did you miss your plane?

A: I made a mistake and turned off my alarm. If I hadn't turned off the alarm, I wouldn't have missed my plane. I would have had the internship. And I would have gotten it, I'm sure.

B: Too bad.

Keep talking!

A logical explanation?

Students A and B

A PAIR WORK You have a picture of a home office AFTER something happened. What do you think might have happened? Think of as many explanations as you can.

B GROUP WORK Join classmates who have a BEFORE picture. Their picture shows the office five minutes before. Tell them what you think might have happened. Then find out what really happened.

A: We think that someone might have . . .

B: Or someone could have . . .

C: Actually, here's what really happened . . .

C PAIR WORK Now you have a BEFORE picture of a restaurant. Describe the scene. What has happened? What's happening?

D GROUP WORK Join classmates who have an AFTER picture. Their picture shows the restaurant five minutes after your picture. Listen to their ideas about what might have happened. Then tell them what really happened.

A logical explanation?

Students C and D

A PAIR WORK You have a BEFORE picture of a home office. Describe the scene. What has happened? What is happening?

B GROUP WORK Join classmates who have an AFTER picture. Their picture shows the office five minutes after your picture. Listen to their ideas about what might have happened. Then tell them what really happened.

A: We think that someone might have . . .

B: Or someone could have . . .

C: Actually, here's what really happened . . .

C PAIR WORK Now you have a picture of a restaurant AFTER something has happened. What do you think might have happened? Think of as many explanations as you can.

D GROUP WORK Join classmates who have a BEFORE picture. Their picture shows the restaurant five minutes before. Tell them what you think might have happened. Then find out what really happened.

Keep talking!

Unsolved mysteries

A GROUP WORK Choose a different picture from others in your group. Read about the picture. How can you explain the unsolved mystery? Take turns. Describe the mystery and answer the questions.

A: There is a manuscript that no one can read.

B: Do you know where it's from?

A: Yes, it's from Italy, but the manuscript isn't in Italian.

C: Do you have any idea if . . . ?

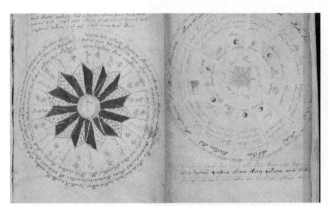

The Voynich manuscript is a book that was written in the 15th or 16th century. The author and alphabet are unknown. The book was discovered in Italy, but the language isn't like any European language. Even modern computers haven't "cracked" the code. Who wrote it, and why?

The Nazca lines are hundreds of "pictures" that were created in the Nazca Desert of Peru. They include birds, fish, spiders, monkeys, llamas, and lizards. How were they made? And why would anyone create such complicated pictures that you can only see from the air?

In the 1930s, workers in the Costa Rican jungle discovered mysterious stone balls that were perfectly round. Some were as small as a tennis ball, but others were larger – very large! They are human-made, but who made them, and how? What were they used for?

In 1947, something crashed near Roswell, New Mexico. At first the U.S. military said it was a "flying disc," but later changed its story and said it was a secret weather balloon. Others believe it was an alien spaceship. They think the government is hiding the truth. What crashed at Roswell?

B CLASS ACTIVITY Describe other unexplained mysteries that you know about. Answer your classmates' questions.

Keep talking!

143

Find the differences

Student A

A PAIR WORK You and your partner have a picture of the same accident. Tell your partner what the witnesses said in your picture. Your partner will report what other witnesses said. Find four differences in their reports.

A: Peter told the police officer that the driver hadn't stopped at the light.

B: Jan also said he hadn't stopped at the light. She said that she'd seen the light turn yellow.

A: But Peter told the police officer he'd seen the light turn red. So that's different.

B PAIR WORK Who do you think are the most reliable witnesses? The least reliable? Why? Whose fault was it – the driver's, the bicyclist's, or both? Why?

Keep talking!

Who said what?

A Write a *yes* / *no* question for each topic.

Topics	Questions	Notes: Who said what?
Work or school		
Entertainment		
Relationships		
Sports		
Past experiences		
Future goals		
other: (your own idea)		

B CLASS ACTIVITY Ask different classmates your questions. Write their names. Take notes on the most interesting answers.

A: Claudia, have you ever arrived to college late?

B: I have. I arrived an hour late once because there was an accident on the highway.

C GROUP WORK Report your most interesting questions and answers.

"I asked Claudia if she'd ever arrived to college late. She told me that she had . . ."

Find the differences

Student B

A PAIR WORK You and your partner have a picture of the same accident. Tell your partner what the witnesses said in your picture. Your partner will report what other witnesses said. Find four differences in their reports.

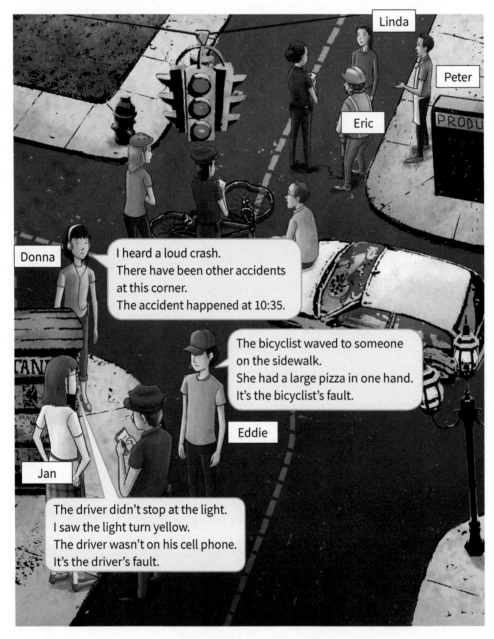

A: Peter told the police officer that the driver hadn't stopped at the light.

B: Jan also said he hadn't stopped at the light. She said that she'd seen the light turn yellow.

A: But Peter told the police officer he'd seen the light turn red. So that's different.

B PAIR WORK Who do you think are the most reliable witnesses? The least reliable? Why? Whose fault was it – the driver's, the bicyclist's, or both? Why?

Convenient services

A PAIR WORK Look at the picture of the shopping mall. Where can you have or get these things done?

get a doctor's prescription filled	have a résumé photocopied
get a passport photo taken	have a skirt made
get photos printed	have a suit cleaned
get your hair cut	have a watch repaired
get your nails done	have your eyes checked
have a computer virus removed	have your glasses fixed

A: You can get a passport photo taken at Picture It.

B: And maybe at Office Works.

B PAIR WORK What else can you get or have done at the places in the picture? Tell your partner.

C PAIR WORK Where do you get or have things done near you? Use the ideas in Part A and ideas of your own.

"I get my hair cut at Hair and Now. It's on Main Street, near my house."

Will that really happen?

A Add three more question topics to the chart about life in the future.

Find someone who believes . . . in the future.	Name
students will be finishing college in just three years	
most people will be eating only organic food	
women will be leading most countries in the world	
ocean levels will rise to dangerous levels	
the world's population will reach 10 billion	
children will work independently in classrooms	
people will be working a 20-hour workweek	
most people will be working until age 70	
most people will be speaking English as a native language	

B `CLASS ACTIVITY` Ask questions and find classmates who believe the possibilities in Part A will be happening in the future. Write their names. Ask questions for more information.

A: In your opinion, will students be finishing college in just three years in the future?

B: Yes, they will.

A: Why do you think that will happen?

B: College will be even more expensive, so students will try to finish college faster.

C `GROUP WORK` Share your opinions about the possibilities in the chart. Do you agree with your classmates?

Keep talking!

The environmental game

PAIR WORK Play the game. Put a small object on Start. Toss a coin.

 Move 1 space.

Heads

 Move 2 spaces.

Tails

Answer the question: "What is being done in the picture?" Use the pictures and the words.

If your answer describes something that helps the environment, move forward one square.

If your answer describes something that hurts the environment, say what needs to be done and stay on the square.

A: Heads. Conserve. Water is being conserved. That helps the environment.

B: Tails. Waste. Energy is being wasted. That doesn't help the environment. The lights need to be turned off.

Keep talking!

Beautification project

A GROUP WORK **Plan a community improvement project. Decide together on a project, and complete the information.**

What you'll make more beautiful:

☐ a park ☐ a road ☐ a playground ☐ a wall
☐ a river ☐ a sidewalk ☐ a building ☐ other: _____

What you'll do:

☐ paint ☐ clean up ☐ rebuild ☐ plant ☐ other: _____

What you'll need:

☐ trash bags ☐ shovels ☐ brooms ☐ paint
☐ flowers / plants ☐ tree ☐ gloves ☐ other: _____

How long it will take: **Who will benefit:**

_____   _____

Who will do which jobs: **What else you'll need to decide:**

_____   _____

A: I think the front of the school needs to be more beautiful.

B: I agree. It looks old, so maybe we could paint it and plant flowers.

C: And if everyone helps, it will be a real school community project.

D: That's a good idea, although we would need to get permission first.

B CLASS ACTIVITY **Share your ideas. Decide on one project. How could you work together to complete the project?**

Keep talking!

Irregular verbs

Base form	Simple past	Past participle
be	was, were	been
become	became	become
begin	began	begun
bite	bit	bitten
break	broke	broken
bring	brought	brought
build	built	built
buy	bought	bought
catch	caught	caught
choose	chose	chosen
come	came	come
cost	cost	cost
cut	cut	cut
do	did	done
draw	drew	drawn
drink	drank	drunk
drive	drove	driven
eat	ate	eaten
fall	fell	fallen
feel	felt	felt
find	found	found
forget	forgot	forgotten
get	got	gotten
give	gave	given
go	went	gone
grow	grew	grown
hang	hung	hung
have	had	had
hear	heard	heard
hold	held	held
hurt	hurt	hurt
keep	kept	kept

Base form	Simple past	Past participle
know	knew	known
leave	left	left
lend	lent	lent
lose	lost	lost
make	made	made
meet	met	met
pay	paid	paid
put	put	put
read	read	read
ride	rode	ridden
run	ran	run
say	said	said
see	saw	seen
sell	sold	sold
send	sent	sent
show	showed	shown
sing	sang	sung
sit	sat	sat
sleep	slept	slept
speak	spoke	spoken
spend	spent	spent
stand	stood	stood
stick	stuck	stuck
swim	swam	swum
take	took	taken
teach	taught	taught
tell	told	told
think	thought	thought
wake	woke	woken
wear	wore	worn
win	won	won
write	wrote	written

Credits

The authors and publishers acknowledge the following sources of copyright material and are grateful for the permissions granted. While every effort has been made, it has not always been possible to identify the sources of all the material used, or to trace all copyright holders. If any omissions are brought to our notice, we will be happy to include the appropriate acknowledgements on reprinting and in the next update to the digital edition, as applicable.

Text
U9: Text adapted from sources https://www.wired.com/2009/03/ff-perfectmemory/ & https://www.theguardian.com/science/2017/feb/08/total-recall-the-people-who-never-forget. Reproduced with kind permissions of Jill Price; **U6:** The Nine Enneagram Type Descriptions are copyrighted by The Enneagram Institute and are used in the Four Corners Second Edition SB4 with permission; **U12:** Text adapted from reproduced "The Fundamentals of El Sistema". Copyright © 2017. Reproduced with the kind permission of Eric Booth.

Photography
All below images are sourced from Getty Images.
U7: ©Original from Gwoeii/Getty images; RunPhoto/DigitalVision; Manakin/iStock Editorial/Getty Images Plus; sborisov/iStock/Getty Images Plus; kapulya/iStock/Getty Images Plus; sborisov/iStock/Getty Images Plus; kapulya/iStock/Getty Images Plus; fotomirc/iStock/Getty Images Plus; Dave King/Dorling Kindersley; LivingImages/iStock/Getty Images Plus; Museum of Science and Industry, Chicago/Archive Photos; ThomasVogel/iStock/Getty Images Plus; ivan-96/iStock/Getty Images Plus; Maxiphoto/iStock Editorial/Getty Images Plus; **U8:** Pekic/E+; Maskot; WALTER ZERLA/Cultura; South_agency/iStock/Getty Images Plus; fizkes/iStock/Getty Images Plus; Hybrid Images/Cultura; Georgethefourth/iStock/Getty Images Plus; MachineHeadz/iStock/Getty Images Plus; Giantstep Inc/Photodisc; PeopleImages/E+; Cultura RM Exclusive/Robin James; dimarik/iStock/Getty Images Plus; Jon Furniss/Wireimage; **U9:** altrendo images/Juice Images; Radius Images; ElleFitz/iStock/Getty Images Plus; lolostock/iStock/Getty Images Plus; Zoonar RF/Getty Images Plus; Bettmann; Dan Tuffs/Getty Images News; **U10:** siur/iStock/Getty Images Plus; paul mansfield photography/Moment; Nine OK/Photographer's Choice; paul mansfield photography/Moment; Paul Mansfield; ; ©Chris Whitehead/Getty images; MARTIN BUREAU/AFP; Ghislain & Marie David de Lossy/The Image Bank; Jon Kopaloff/FilmMagic; **U11:** braverabbit/iStock/Getty Images Plus; Eco/Universal Images Group; YakobchukOlena/iStock/Getty Images Plus; cyano66/iStock/Getty Images Plus; Kim Steele/Photodisc; warrengoldswain/iStock/Getty Images Plus; BJI/Blue Jean Images; NicoElNino/iStock/Getty Images Plus; Giulio_Fornasar/iStock/Getty Images Plus; ©Stephen Derr/Getty images; Lisa-Blue/iStock/Getty Images Plus; Dave and Les Jacobs/Lloyd Dobbie/Blend Images; ; Hero Images; aluxum/E+; Hero Images; isitsharp/iStock/Getty Images Plus; Viaframe/Corbis; **U12:** Maik Mitschke/EyeEm; Toa55/iStock/Getty Images Plus; ©Spencer Platt/Getty images; John Seaton Callahan/Moment; Frederic Cirou/PhotoAlto Agency RF Collections; Tetra Images; Photick/Sigrid Olsson/Getty Images Plus; bariskaradeniz/iStock/Getty Images Plus; asiseeit/E+; Blend Images - KidStock/Brand X Pictures; JackF/iStock/Getty Images Plus; bbostjan/iStock/Getty Images Plus; ; JUAN BARRETO/AFP; Simon Jarratt/Corbis/VCG/Getty Images; **End Matter:** Yiu Yu Hoi/DigitalVision; Chris Beall/Lonely Planet Images; David Zaitz/Photonica; izusek/E+; g-stockstudio/iStock/Getty Images Plus; g-stockstudio/iStock/Getty Images Plus; RuslanGuzov/iStock/Getty Images Plus; 81a/Photolibrary/Stockbyte/Getty Images Plus; sergey02/iStock/Getty Images Plus; Westend61; DoucetPh/iStock Editorial/Getty Images Plus; Studioofcrayons/iStock/Getty Images Plus; Image Source/Photodisc; marugod83/iStock/Getty Images Plus; Clerkenwell/Vetta; Monty Rakusen/Cultura; airdone/iStock/Getty Images Plus; Times/Getty Images.

Front cover by VisitBritain; Hero Images; Patchareeporn Sakoolchai/Moment.
Back cover by Monty Rakusen/Cultura.
The following images are sourced from other libraries:
U7: ©Lukas Miglinas/Alamy; ©The Image Works; ©National Geographic; Andreblais/Dreamstime; Kyodo News/Newscom; Ed Bailey/AP Photo; **U8:** F.G.I CO., LTD./Alamy; **U9:** ©Frank Veronsky; **U10:** ©Kip Evans/Alamy; **U11:** ©Kip Evans/Alamy; **U12:** MAISANT Ludovic/hemis/Age Fotostock; ©Frank Veronsky; **End Matter:** © US mint; ©Courtesy of Think Geek; Messy Desk Design LLC; ©Bupkes Bakery; ©Ant Works; ©Motorcycle Mojo Magazine; ©Clever Care; Art Collection 2/Alamy; Carver Mostardi/Media Bakery; ©Manor Photography/Alamy.

Illustration
Front Matter: Kim Johnson; **U7:** QBS Learning; Kim Johnson; **U9:** Dani Geremia/Beehive Illustration; QBS Learning; Belgin Wedman; **U10–11:** QBS Learning; **End Matter:** Szilvia Szakall/Beehive Illustration; Dani Geremia/Beehive Illustration; Kim Johnson; QBS Learning.

Art direction, book design, and layout services: QBS Learning
Audio production: CityVox, NYC and John Marshall Media
Video production: Steadman Productions